Praise for The 52-Week Life Passion Project

The 52-Week Life Passion Project *includes a year's worth of powerful, actionable exercises to help you discover and live your passion. It's insightful, practical, and creative—a great tool for transformation and growth!*

 Lori Deschene, Founder of tinybuddha.com and author of *Tiny Buddha: Simple Wisdom for Life's Hard Questions*

The 52-Week Life Passion Project *is the first step on an entirely new life's journey— a life filled with passion and joy and accomplishment. It will help awaken your true inner self and rekindle your love for life. You owe it to yourself to read this book.*

 Corbett Barr, entrepreneur and founder of ThinkTraffic.net

This book is a gem. As you move through it, week after week, you become the project. You answer questions—some not so easy, but I think that's Barrie's intention—to guide you towards your life passion, one challenging question at a time, so that you begin to truly understand where you are, how you got there and what might be holding you back from being somewhere else—somewhere that seems entirely reachable with Barrie's book in hand.

 Katie Tallo, writer and filmmaker, katietallo.com

Few things are as important as knowing your passion in life, and few people are as gifted at helping others discover their calling in life as Barrie Davenport. With her years of experience, breakthroughs and insights, and masterful Weekly Actions, discovering your true passion in life is finally within reach. Barrie has drawn the map. Now it's up to you to follow where it leads.

 Jason Gracia, author of *Motivated in Minutes*, JasonGracia.com

Barrie's book is a treasure trove of information to help you clarify, identify, and overcome your fears to start following your passions in life. The wonderful section on understanding yourself is a fantastic primer to realising your potential and finally take action to live your passion. It took me six years to find and follow my passion, and I consider myself very fortunate, this book will get you there much quicker. For anybody who has ever wanted to live life on their own terms, then you need this book.

 Steven Aitchison, Author of *100 Ways to D~~~*

I've always believed that one of the causes of illness, discontent, and even depression is living life without passion. More to the point, we aren't living our personal passion, the thing that makes us prick up our ears, lean forward in our seats and eagerly want to live. Barrie Davenport's The 52-Week Life Passion Project, writes with remarkable clarity, heartwarming honesty and delightful creativity, is critical for anyone who wants to live a life filled with passion. This is not a dry "how to" book. This book is not only highly practical, but refreshingly inspirational. The reader senses that Barrie Davenport "walks her talk" and has actively been down road that leads to passion.

     ✎ Robin Easton, author of *Naked in Eden*

Barrie takes you on a step-by-step journey to living a life that brings you joy and passion. This well-written guide is easy to digest with weekly bite-size actions and reflections. In this guide, Barrie has prepared a way for your passion to simmer to the surface for you to grasp.

     ✎ Marci Payne, Licensed Professional Counselor, Liberating Choices

The 52-Week Life Passion Project is life changing and life affirming! Barrie is a brilliant writer who models beautifully how we can all tap into our passion and begin living our dreams. It's comprehensive without being overwhelming. The weekly action steps will help you uncover your gifts so that you can start sharing them with the world! This book is a must have for anyone who is ready to embrace their life fully and who dares to make their dreams come true!

     ✎ Jodi Chapman, author of *Soul Speak*, the *Soulful Journals* series, and *Coming Back to Life*

Discover your life's passion in one year—that's the promise made by Barrie Davenport, author of The 52-Week Life Passion Project. From defining success, to claiming balance to financial freedom, Barrie lays out a simple week-by-week plan that will bring more peace, contentment and focus into your life. The book is powerful in its ability to transform your life while discovering your life's passion.

     ✎ Alex Blackwell, Founder of The BridgeMaker.com

THE 52-WEEK LIFE PASSION PROJECT

The 52-Week
Life Passion Project

by Barrie Davenport

Blue Elephant Press
Raleigh, NC

Barrie Davenport
permission@BarrieDavenport.com
www.BarrieDavenport.com

Published by:
Blue Elephant Press
info@blueelephantpress.com
www.blueelephantpress.com

To Allyn, John and Diana

Contents

Introduction

Don't ask yourself what the world needs;
ask yourself what makes you come alive.
And then go and do that. Because what
the world needs is people who have
come alive.

<ᗍ Harold Whitman

Life passion is a powerful thing. It can transform you from someone who is simply living life to someone who is in love with life. It can change your perspective about everything, the same way putting on sunglasses adds brilliant clarity and sparkle to a sunny day.

Finding your life passion is like finally coming home after being a stranger in a strange land. You are at peace, happily content, and fully engaged.

By finding and living your passion, life problems and difficulties don't disappear instantly; but it does change the way you perceive and handle them. When something exciting is happening in one part of your life, the problems in other areas don't seem so over-whelming. You have more emotional energy and creative resources to deal with them. And you want to deal with them quickly so you can return to doing what you love.

I know these things because I spent most of my adult life without a clear passion. It wasn't until I reached mid-life and was forced to reassess everything about my life that I realized I had to take action. My inner self was screaming so loudly for change that I couldn't take it any longer. I had to find something that made me come alive or else shrivel up and blow away.

I spent over twenty years as a successful public relations profes-sional, helping my clients realize their own passions by positioning them for success. As the marketing and PR director for a network of career colleges, I supported students as they pursued their own career passions. My focus had always been on helping others reach their dreams and fulfill their personal callings.

Over the course of several years, I knew something was missing in my life. I knew that in spite of all of the blessings in my life—a loving family, beautiful children, a successful career—there was a hole inside of me. Something vital was missing. At the time, I couldn't pinpoint exactly what I was seeking, but my restlessness was sending me a strong message from deep inside.

I'd spent years helping others reach their dreams and live their passions. I'd seen how passion can energize and transform people. I'd stood by the side of actors, artists, dancers, politicians, designers, students and business professionals as their passions propelled them to success and happiness. I knew the raw power of passion. I loved helping others on their passion journeys, but it made me realize that I was missing that same passion in my own life. I felt like I was on the sidelines, watching something amazing but not participating in it.

After my oldest child left home (always a watershed life event), I finally took the time and space to figure it out. I forced myself to stop believing the lies and limitations I'd clung to for so many years about myself and my abilities. I knew this was the only way I could move forward unhindered.

My struggle on the path to discovery was long and circuitous. I didn't have a road map. I often found myself wondering if there was something wrong with me, if I simply didn't have the capacity to be fulfilled and live passionately.

After this lengthy process of self-discovery—including much research, reading, workshops, assessment tests and coaching—I discovered that my passion was working closely with people as a personal coach, helping them define and create the best possible life for themselves. During this time, I also discovered an intense love for writing and blogging.

Through my own experience in finding my passion, coupled with decades of work in PR supporting my clients' passions, I uncovered the necessary steps to lead others on the path of self-discovery. Through my work as a coach, I learned to present my knowledge in a way that makes it far easier for others seeking their life passion than it was for me during my own search. This knowledge is what I'm presenting here in *The 52-Week Life Passion Project*.

The purpose of this book is to help you transform yourself and your life so that one year from today, you will be well on the way to a passionate new life—however you define that for yourself. Along the way, you will gain much more clarity on who you are, what you want from life and what is holding you back. You will also streamline and balance your life so that you have the space and energy to pursue and fully enjoy your life passion.

Every week for fifty-two weeks, you will take small and manageable steps. Each step peels back the layers of self-awareness followed by specific actions that keep you moving forward week after week to a passionate life.

Passion Project Suggestions

Every person reading this book is standing at a different crossroad in their life. Some of you may need an infusion of passion to round out an already good life. Others may be deeply unhappy with their current life and want a complete overhaul.

Some may have all of the elements of a passionate life at their disposal right now, but they are stuck and confused about how to use those elements and transform their lives.

Through these fifty-two weeks, this project covers four main areas:

> ⊱ Understanding more about yourself;
>
> ⊱ Addressing roadblocks and limitations that hold you back;
>
> ⊱ Creating a vision for a passionate new life;
>
> ⊱ Taking actions that will make that vision real.

You may find that some of the weekly lessons and actions don't apply to your life right now. But I encourage you to read the lessons and take the actions anyway. You will still benefit from the added clarity this self-work provides, and you may find the information you uncover about yourself leads you to something unexpected and exciting.

As you encounter the weekly lessons dealing with limitations, emotional barriers, and fears, you may feel uncomfortable or even sad. I encourage you to be completely honest with yourself and about yourself. The truth provides valid information that can reveal why you haven't been able to find or live your passion so far. Quite often, our internal world is the only thing holding us back from living passionately. We need to deal with these internal limitations before we can find our passion.

You may be tempted to read ahead, trying to cram fifty-two weeks of learning and actions into less time. Believe me, I understand that. Who wants to wait a year to live passionately?

But I encourage you to try and begin this book with the mindset that the project itself will be your passion for the next fifty-two weeks. Each of the weekly actions requires time, introspection and reflection. Much of the change and transformation occurs during the days when you *aren't* reading. Give yourself the gift of this time and fully complete the process.

All of the weekly actions require writing and reflection, so please use *The 52-Week Life Passion Project Workbook* or another journal to chronicle your thoughts and progress.

You will frequently refer back to your answers from previous weeks, so this writing is a critical part of the process. It is the only way to get the most from this passion project.

More than anything, I hope you will begin this project with excitement and anticipation. You are embarking on a journey that can only lead to positive change in your life. By this time next year, you will know more about what makes you come alive with joy, and what gives your life meaning and purpose. You will be well on the way to making this your daily reality. A passionate new life is waiting for you. It's time to go claim it!

Week 1:
What's Nagging at You?

Here you are—reading this book about life passion. There's a reason you picked up it. There's a reason why you're interested in life passion. The words themselves sound enticing and sexy . . . life passion. It sounds like something that could transform you in some profound and mysterious way. Everyone wants it. Some people claim to have it. But most of us have no idea what *life passion* is or how to go about getting it. Most of us are trapped in our humdrum existence.

I'm sure you've crossed paths with passionate people in your life. They exude an aura of enthusiasm and positivity. They are purposeful and engaged in what they are doing. They may not be wealthy or highly successful in the traditional sense (*although wealth and success may be by-products of their passion*).

But they are clearly happy and satisfied. No, they are more than satisfied—they are passionate about what they have going on in their lives.

They are no more lucky, intelligent or creative than you are. The only difference between you and these passionate people is that they've figured out their passion and have done something to make it a big part of their lives. But you have plenty of time to catch up.

The first step toward any positive change—any personal growth or transformation—is awareness. Your first step toward life passion is the awareness that your life isn't what you want it to be. That's probably why you're reading this book. Whether you realize it or not, a budding awareness has already taken shape in you. You are now already on the path to your life passion.

This awareness might take the form of a vague sense of dissatisfaction. You may have feelings of uneasiness or unhappiness with your life or work. You might feel depressed, bored, or restless far too often. You simply don't feel content, fulfilled, purposeful or entirely happy.

Perhaps you've been in this mode of seeking for some time, not really sure what you are looking for. Maybe you've attempted a few new activities or career moves, but it all feels scattered and directionless. You're not sure exactly what you want or how to gain clarity about that. You may have even come to the conclusion there simply isn't a right fit for you—there isn't anything that will make you feel *passionate* about life.

But there is. All of these negative emotions and directionless struggles are evidence that there is something more for you. Your psyche—your inner self—knows that something isn't right and won't be satisfied until you do something about it. As hard as you may have tried to make yourself happy with the status quo, the real you who deeply longs for something more will not be pushed aside and ignored.

It's time to listen to your inner self and take action. And now you have some direction and guidance to help you. So have faith. Your life passion is inside of you, just waiting to be uncovered. Now it's your job to do the work that will uncover it forever.

Weekly Action

What is nagging at you? What feelings or thoughts are you having that indicate there is something more, something that will make you come alive? How is your life passion knocking on the door of your soul, asking to be uncovered? What awareness do you have about your desire to find your life passion?

Write down your thoughts about these questions, even if you don't completely understand everything you are feeling or thinking.

Week 2:
Childhood Joy

It's never too late to have a happy childhood.

      ↄ Tom Robbins, *Still Life with Woodpecker*

When you were a child, you didn't think about your life passion. You just lived it. You didn't think about whether you were happy, fulfilled, living a life of purpose. You were in the moment—learning, exploring, playing, laughing, crying, discovering the world around you.

If you had a fairly normal upbringing, your purpose and passion were defined by the very essence of childhood. When you were engaged in play and discovery, you were "in the flow." Time disappeared—at least until mom called you in for dinner or the school bell rang.

Can you remember that time in your life? Can you remember how joyful and free it felt to be a child, without responsibilities, expectations or self-doubt?

When you uncover your life passion and begin to live it, that's how you can feel again—maybe not 24/7, but at least for as long as you are engaged in your passionate work or play. And even after you stop, the enthusiasm and joy of the passion will linger around you and sustain you until you re-engage and return to the flow.

In fact, living your life passion has a way of transforming every aspect of your life. Everything begins to work in synergy to support and expand your passion.

That's how powerful life passion is—just the memory of it, the anticipation of it, will make you happy . . . even giddy. Maybe you'll rush through dinner to get back to it. Maybe you'll wake up and remember with excitement that it's there waiting for you, like a shiny, new pair of shoes.

Maybe you will daydream about it—just like you did when you were a kid and you couldn't wait to get back out there and finish the fort, ride your bike or swing high up into the air.

Being a child is the ultimate in passionate living. And if this was encouraged by your parents, you had the freedom to experiment, get dirty and explore all of the possibilities that life had to offer you.

Our adult lives have added layers of responsibilities, stresses and disappointments. We've grown far, far away from the simple, pure passions of childhood. Can you remember those feelings? Maybe it's time to be a child again.

Weekly Action

Close your eyes and breathe in and out for a count of ten. When you feel peaceful and calm, and with your eyes closed, go back to your childhood.

Think about some of your happiest childhood memories—when you were in the flow, lost in time because you were so engaged in the moment. What were you doing? How did it feel? What did you love about those moments and events?

Describe those moments and tease out the elements of each that brought you the most profound joy.

Week 3:
Childhood Limitations

Hopefully your childhood was healthy and happy. Hopefully your parents were loving, supportive, encouraging and emotionally mature. Hopefully you were allowed to explore, play and discover the world around you without shaming, criticism or unnecessary restrictions.

When this isn't the case—when something disrupts the child's ability to feel safe, light-hearted, secure, confident, supported or loved—then his passionate and unfettered play and normal emotional development is stunted.

Bad and fearful feelings become associated with self-discovery or with life in general. Things get serious. The child becomes hyper-vigilant, waiting for cues from the all-powerful adults to reveal what is accepted, what is pleasing, what is expected. Sometimes things are really bad, and the passions of childhood slip away entirely.

Even in the healthiest families, as a child grows older, goes to school and interacts with peers, the unabashed passion that once defined her is now tempered by expectations, subtle shaming or criticisms.

Over time, you might even begin to believe what you are told about yourself. You might begin to believe that you aren't creative, smart, pretty, funny, worthy or any number of other limiting beliefs that have come to define you and alter your choices and behavior.

You stuffed these beliefs into your little Spiderman backpack and carried them with you, all the way through adolescence, young adulthood, into your career, your marriage, your life.

They've become a part of you, such a part of you that you might not realize they are no longer true or necessary. Haven't you outgrown that little backpack? Maybe those beliefs don't really fit you anymore. Maybe you don't have to be that person.

Consider what life would be like for you if all of those ancient beliefs about yourself simply disappeared. You are now a blank slate where all possibilities are valid options for you. There's nothing holding you back from being or trying anything.

Weekly Action

How did those around you (*parents, teachers, peers, etc.*) impact your childhood passions? Were your passions and interests supported and encouraged or stunted in some way? What did "those in power" tell you about yourself as a child that has limited you, made you fearful or held you back? Write down these limitations and what you might have done as a child if you weren't held back for some reason.

What passionate activities would you have pursued if only . . . ?

Week 4:
What's Changed Since Childhood?

Beliefs have the power to create and the power to destroy. Human beings have the awesome ability to take any experience of their lives and create a meaning that disempowers them or one that can literally save their lives.

— Tony Robbins

So you've been carrying that Spiderman backpack with you for years now, filled with old beliefs and limitations. It's almost a part of your body, like the purse you throw over your shoulder or the belt you put on without thinking about it.

But when was the last time you unzipped the backpack and looked inside? When was the last time you actually reached inside of the backpack, pulled out one of those beliefs to see if it still holds water or just holds you down?

Once upon a time, maybe you weren't the first one picked for the team. Maybe you weren't a great artist or didn't make straight A's. Or perhaps someone told you that you weren't good enough at something.

There were things you wanted to try, but didn't because you were criticized about the things you did attempt.

But that was then. You aren't ten anymore. Your parents or teachers or peers don't make the rules. They don't define you or your abilities. They have no real power over you anymore (*unless, of course, you give it to them*). You've done a lot of living, growing and learning since then. You have a lot of time and experience under your belt.

Yet you still carry around that backpack full of limiting beliefs, fears and untested abilities. Who says you can't? Who says it's not worth a try? Who says you will fail? And so what if you do? What a silly bunch of junk you've been toting around all of these years. What a worthless collection of old bones you've stored in that backpack.

One of the greatest blessings of life is that growth, learning and change are neither linear nor stagnant. You didn't lose your chance forever because it didn't happen when you were a child or young adult. You aren't relegated to *no you can't* now because you rarely heard *yes you can* back in the day.

You have endless opportunities for change and renewal, for discovering new abilities or old ones you thought were dried up or worthless. You have unlimited do-overs in life.

So open that backpack. Spread those beliefs out on the table in the light of day, like old bones dug up from a sand pit. Look at them, all shriveled and sad. They don't have power over you. Why are you carrying those old bones around? Clean them out. In fact, throw the entire thing away. You've outgrown Spiderman anyway. When you challenge those old bones, they will crumble into dust. They no longer hold truth for you. Now you can start fresh. Now you can be a child again, with a fresh new slate, even if you have to pretend for a while.

It's OK to pretend, because eventually you'll forget you're pretending. Then you'll just be living . . . with passion.

Weekly Action

Write down every one of the limiting beliefs and fears you've carried from childhood. Are they still true for you or even partially true? Really? How are they not true? What is the evidence you have from today, this time of your life, that they are no longer true?

Become a detective and find the evidence that your old beliefs are old bones—they crumble when challenged. Write down the evidence and refer to it often.

Week 5:
Your Beliefs About Passion

It's been a long time since you were a child. But those childhood experiences set the foundation for your hopes and dreams as an adult. If things were good, or at least fairly normal in childhood, you started with a solid foundation—a platform from which to spring into adulthood with the promise that you can be whatever you want to be.

The world is your oyster.

If things weren't so great (*or if they were awful*), you were too busy coping or simply surviving to entertain the possibility of finding your passion.

You just wanted to find the door, the exit ramp to freedom, the escape hatch to a place that was pain free.

A healthy, happy childhood provides a leg up. It launches you with security, a certain level of self-confidence and bright expectations. A difficult childhood can launch you with a deficit in these things which may require more work on self-confidence and self-esteem as you work toward your life passion.

Either way, there is more that contributes to finding your passion than just your childhood experiences. Your temperament and personality, relationships, life circumstances, education and level of self-awareness all help shape your beliefs about yourself, your abilities, your hopes and your dreams.

Everything we've done in life—every experience and relationship—adds to or diminishes our belief that life passion is possible and our awareness of what our passions might be.

Hopefully the outcome of all of these life experiences is a sense that your passion is within you, just waiting to be uncovered and explored. Or perhaps the outcome up until now has been a belief that you have no life passion and that searching for one is a waste of time.

In order to start the process of finding and living your passion, you will need to challenge yourself and your preconceived ideas. You need to start with a blank slate and remain open to all possibilities, no matter how ridiculous or impossible they may seem.

You have an outdated belief system tarred with the gunk of childhood beliefs, years of experiences and useless entrenched thinking. It's time to pour some goo remover on that belief system.

Bring it back down to zero-base, to a clean palette where you are open to create some brand new mental and emotional energy. This week, give yourself permission to abandon all beliefs and limitations you've constructed about yourself. We are about to create a new life paradigm.

Weekly Action

Think about your current beliefs related to finding and having a life passion. Do you believe it is possible to have a life passion? Do you believe it is worthwhile to look for it?

Write down all of your current ideas and beliefs about finding and living your life passion. Are you willing to dismiss, or at least back-burner, those ideas for now? Can you start fresh with no pre-conceived notions?

Week 6:
Resistance and Fear

Do the thing you fear most and the death
of fear is certain.

~ Mark Twain

When you look at your beliefs about a life passion, you might stir
the pot of fears within. You might feel a certain resistance around
beginning this work of transformation and self-creation.

It is scary. Change is scary—even positive change.

An internal wall starts to form before you really have a chance
to think things through. Tightness builds in your chest. A bit of

shallowness is in each breath. A defeated feeling emerges before you've even begun.

"This is stupid. Why am I doing this? Things are OK. Things are fine. I just need to be happy with the way things are."

Doesn't it feel strange to be so unhappy, even hating our lives, and yet still cling to the status quo when presented with the opportunity to change? The devil we know appears safer than the unknown passion beyond the resistance.

So far, you've been coping with this dreary life. You are managing well with mediocre. You've been pretty satisfied with pretty good. Now that you've put your foot on the path to change, you might be wondering whether this is a good time to hightail it back to safe ground.

When you started this passion work, you began lifting up stones. You see the nastiness underneath—the creepy crawly things, the worms and bugs. Your first reaction is to drop the stone and cover it back up. Who wants to deal with that hot mess?

But if you lift the stone again, you may discover the creepy crawly things (*your fears*) are pretty harmless. They won't bite you. In fact, when exposed to the light of day, they often run away or disappear.

That's the thing about fears. They can cause a lot of resistance (*that's their only power*). But when you challenge them, expose them to truth, see them for what they are—they almost always go away.

Then resistance loosens up. Then you are able to start with a clean slate. You are open to the flow of ideas and inspiration. When you challenge just one little fear—just one creepy crawly thing—you feel empowered. It's not so bad. It's never as bad as you fear it will be. It's mostly just the *feeling* of fear that scares us. The reality is manageable.

Weekly Action

Where do you feel resistance around finding and living your life passion? Where and how are you pushing back against doing this creative work? What fears are attached to your resistance?

Complete the following sentence as many times as you can until you run out of answers: "I am showing resistance to finding my passion by . . . "

Now do the same for this statement: "I am resistant because I am afraid that . . . "

Week 7:
The Fear Challenge

Throughout this 52-week project of finding and living your passion, you will encounter fears. You will begin with them. They will follow you through the process (*but might mutate and put on disguises*), and they will give you one or two more jabs before you settle into a new life.

You can't let that stop you. You must not let that stop you. Fear is up to tricky business, but you are smarter and more capable than fear will allow you to believe. Fear is like the carnivorous plant, Seymour, in *The Little Shop of Horrors*—"Feed me! Feed me!"

Fear and resistance feed on your attention. The more you believe they are real and have power over you, the more powerful they become.

Your challenge through these weeks is to constantly challenge fear. Expect fear. Expect resistance. They like you. They like you even more because you are uncovering them and shrieking in horror.

They are hoping to win the battle against your higher self, against that spark within you that is longing for a passionate life. Fear stays quiet only when you stay put.

A passionate life has no room for fear and resistance. So expect quite a fight from fear. Fear is going to give you a lot of push-back. So now you know. Now you can prepare for the fight.

Like a warrior going into battle, you can arm yourself against fear and resistance. You can shine your saber and put on your breast-plate of courage. You can kneel before the queen of passion and ask for a blessing, a token before you begin your pilgrimage.

Hold that token in your heart—it represents your new passionate life.

However, even when you win one battle, don't allow yourself to get lazy against fear and resistance. You may think they have disap-peared, only to find they launch a surprise attack when you least expect it. Keep your sword handy, your tools well-oiled. Stay on alert.

How does one do battle against fear and resistance? There are many ways, but the boldest is to march forward into the face of fear.

Fear will take on the disguise of a powerful, monstrous beast attempting to scare you away. But just keep marching toward it.

Fear will slither at your feet like a serpent, poisoning your enthusiasm and determination. But just march straight into it.

Fear will hold up resistance like a metal shield, but just push back against it.

What you will learn (*but only truly believe once you've experienced it*) is that fear crumbles in the face of a challenge. Fear *appears* strong, but it is really very weak.

Your heart may be pounding, your eyes may fill with tears, every fiber of your being might scream to turn and run. But don't. Keep moving forward and stare fear in the eye.

Transformation is another weapon you can use against fear. You have the power to transform fear into something useful. Convert the energy of fear to generate fuel for excitement, creativity, experimentation and enthusiasm.

Don't call fear by its name (*thus giving it power*). Don't acknowledge it as fear when you feel it in your gut, in your breathing and your thoughts.

Call it energy. Call it power. Call it a passion incubator. And then transform it into action.

"I am feeling this energy, and I will use it to test the waters, to make that first phone call, to learn more about that job opportunity, to write down my life vision." Use the fear energy to take action.

Come to view fear as a reminder that you are doing the work, stirring the pot, beginning the creation process. Turn fear on its head and use it to empower yourself. That's the fear challenge you will undertake throughout your search, starting this week.

Face it. March past it. Transform it. You hold the power over fear.

Weekly Action

How can you prepare yourself for the inevitability of fear and resistance? What can you do to challenge fear and to reframe it into something useful in this process of finding your passion?

Write down some ideas and practical actions you can take when fear and resistance creep in or launch a surprise attack. Keep your actions handy so you can reach for them when needed.

Week 8:
A Clean Emotional House

Feelings are much like waves, we can't stop them from coming but we can choose which one to surf.

~ Jonatan Mårtensson

No one said this passion work would be easy. But even *the process* of finding your passion will create countless other benefits in your life. This process forces you to do a massive life clean-up—a lovely extra perk of your passion project.

Have you ever planned a fabulous party, something you've eagerly anticipated for months? You anticipate it will be an amazing event with special friends, lots of laughter, music, great food and wonderful energy. You can just imagine how fun it's going to be on the big day. But then you look around and realize your house is a mess. Everything is in disarray. You aren't prepared for the party. You can't invite people over until things are in order.

Well, you can't have a life passion party without having your internal house in order. You can't find your passion, much less live it, if you are a mess.

So go grab a broom and a dustpan. Put on your gloves. It's time to get to work. Look around your internal house. What do you see? What elements of your life are out-of-place, out-of-balance? Where are your emotions right now?

The typical emotional dust bunnies and minor messes are to be expected. General frustrations, occasional stresses, situational sadness or anger are all part of everyday life.

But some emotional messes must be thoroughly cleaned before you can host a passion party. Negative emotions that are sticking around for longer than you care to admit will ruin your passion party. Lingering emotions, such as depression, anger, resentment, anxiety, indecisiveness, fear, bitterness, restlessness, sadness or dread, will sabotage your efforts to find and live your passion. With every step forward, your negative emotions will drag you back down. They will sit on you like a heavy blanket, suffocating your desire, motivation and best intentions.

This isn't the time to throw in the towel. Please don't assume that negative emotions mean you are passionless or that you don't have the ability and energy to find it. Negative emotions are symptoms. They are clues that something isn't in balance for you. They are invitations for healing and growth.

View this awareness as one of the most important steps on your passion journey. Your emotions are telling you something important about yourself. Find the answer, take action to restore healthy emotions, and you've cleared the way to proceed on your passion journey.

Weekly Action

Find a moment where you can sit with your emotions for ten to fifteen minutes. Quiet your mind and try to step outside of yourself, as if you are another person observing you and how you are feeling.

What emotions are you experiencing now? What emotions have you been experiencing over the last few weeks or months? Have any of these been negative emotions that have debilitated you in some way? Write down your answers and thoughts.

Week 9:
Restoring Emotional Equilibrium

There are a myriad of reasons why our emotions get out of whack. Life stresses, disappointments and frustrations can lead to anxiety. Too much anxiety or sadness can cause depression.

Relationship issues burden us with worry, doubt and hurt. Situations or people over which we have little or no control make us feel angry and confused.

And sometimes, out of the blue, a negative emotion waltzes in like an uninvited guest and takes up residence in your psyche. There are no obvious culprits for triggering these emotions, but darned if they don't stick to you like a bad rash.

Why do we get these surprise attacks of undesirable feelings?

Who knows exactly. It could be one of a host of reasons that aren't immediately obvious or measurable.

These might include . . .

- hormonal imbalances or changes

- brain chemistry fluctuations

- food allergies

- lack of sleep

- too much sleep

- a reaction to eating or drinking too much

- unacknowledged stress

- unmet expectations or needs

- a subtle reminder of something sad or frustrating

- the weather or the season

- the mood of the people around you

- the onset of a cold or other illness

- an environmental factor

- an emotional trigger to old wounds or anger

- lingering feelings from a bad dream or from reading or watching something negative

Begin to pay attention to patterns of emotional distress to see if there is a correlation to a cause. If the cause is obvious, do whatever you can to remove or lessen it. Get more sleep. Don't eat foods that bother you. Deal with stress. Spend less time with people who drain or disrupt you. Don't watch or read negative or violent shows or books.

You can also restore emotional equilibrium through self-care like exercise, meditation, proper diet, walking in nature, spending time with supportive friends and practicing positive affirmations.

Even staying highly focused on an engaging activity will help you forget about your negative emotions. Avoid ruminating or over-thinking.

Sometimes we stuff our emotions and pretend we aren't feeling them. *"If I don't acknowledge them, maybe they will go away."*

But they tend to pop back up in other unpleasant ways—physical ailments, depression or anxiety.

It takes a lot of energy to live with negative emotions and even more to pretend they don't exist, leaving few reserves to pursue your passion.

If negative emotions have been lingering for more than a few weeks, it's time to take action and treat them before they become debilitating. Making the decision to visit a professional—either your doctor or a counselor—to help restore your emotional equilibrium is a proactive, positive step. It is a decision that comes from strength, not weakness.

Get to the root of your emotional turmoil and take proactive steps to address it. Once you do, you will have the emotional energy to focus on your passion.

Weekly Action

What do you believe are the root causes of your emotional disequilibrium? What does your intuition tell you about the best way to heal these emotions?

Are you ready to take a step to do that today? What practical action will you take today to restore your emotional balance?

Week 10:
Understanding Your Personality

Always be yourself, express yourself, have
faith in yourself, do not go out and look
for a successful personality and duplicate
it.

⌣ Bruce Lee

There is someone you have lived with for a long time, but how well
do you know them? There's someone whose face has stared back at
you in the mirror, whose voice you hear in your head, whose daily
actions you support with body and mind. Yes, this person is you. But
do you know with certainty what motivates and inspires you? Have
you made acquaintance with yourself?

It's easy to talk about yourself based on your roles in life—what you do, what defines you, what your beliefs are. But what is driving all of that? Why do you behave and think and view the world the way you do?

During this passion project, begin to see yourself as a private detective. One of your first assignments is to learn as much about your subject (*you*) as you possibly can. You want to create an in-depth profile of yourself, delving into the inner workings of what makes you tick.

Why is this important? Because this exploration will give you clues about your natural instincts—the behaviors, traits, interests and emotions that characterize you.

When you learn these things about yourself, you will begin to see patterns emerge and understand why you prefer certain ways of engaging in the world around you.

As a private detective investigating yourself, you need some tools to help you explore and better understand the person you, and those around you, see on the outside (and what you might be feeling on the inside). A personality assessment is an excellent tool to begin this process.

These assessments are created to provide insight into one's psychological make-up and character. They reveal different characteristics or traits that we otherwise might not be aware of or completely understand. They are frequently used in career planning and counseling, as well as employee placement and development.

When you take a personality test and review the results, you will recognize traits in yourself that you may have previously misunderstood or taken for granted.

You will better understand how your personality type impacts your relationships, your career choices and your interests. This information will provide more clues and information as you proceed on your passion search, helping you focus on what supports your natural personality tendencies.

But remember that these test results are only one indicator and shouldn't be relied on as an absolute definition of who you are or what you want in life. Your unique character is far more complex and fluid than the results of a personality test can reveal. The results provide clues and insights but not the final answer.

Weekly Action

Begin some research on personality assessments such as the Myers-Briggs (MBTI), the Keirsey Temperament Sorter and the Strong Interest Inventory.

Take one or more of these assessments (there are free versions of all available online), and read over your personality type results.

What do you see that resonates with you? What personality traits stand out as most natural and reflective of you? Make notes about your insights.

Week 11:
How Are You Smart?

Remember back in elementary school when the teacher was sorting the children in your class, pulling out some students for accelerated classes and moving others into the on-level or remedial groups?

Although the teacher attempted to do this discreetly, everyone in the classroom knew what was going on. The "smart" kids were sorted into one group, the "average" kids were put in another, and the "dumb" kids were placed in a different group.

The smart group worked on advanced material, the average kids work with on-level assignments, and the remedial group struggled to catch up. Everyone knew their place in the academic pecking order.

From those earliest days, a label was stuck to our foreheads defining us (at least in our own minds) as bright, average or stupid. And these labels often followed us into adulthood, reinforced by the traditional measurements of intelligence in higher academic institutions and the work force.

For the last century, intelligence has been primarily measured and expressed by a single number, such as an IQ score. The score reveals one's general intelligence—the ability to think about ideas, analyze situations and solve problems. The belief here is that underlying general intelligence influences performance on all cognitive tasks.

However, the validity of these types of intelligence measurements tests has been challenged in recent years on the basis that they do not cater to all types of people—people of different races, ethnicities and classes especially. Rather, they seem to be greatly based on exposure and knowledge of ideas taught in formal schools.

A new theory of intelligence has emerged in the last thirty years, thanks to Howard Gardner, a developmental psychologist and professor of Cognition and Education in the Harvard Graduate School of Education at Harvard University. Gardner developed the theory of multiple intelligence—a model that differentiates intelligence into various specific modalities, rather than being dominated by a single general ability.

In fact, Gardner suggests there is a wide range of cognitive abilities with only very weak correlations among them. These include:

Spatial: the potential to solve spatial problems, visualize uses of space through imagination, and recognize patterns of space.

Linguistic: keen sensitivity to spoken and written language, the ability to learn languages, and possession of highly developed oral and written communication skills.

Logical-mathematical: strong ability to analyze problems logically, perform mathematical operations, and investigate issues scientifically.

Bodily-kinesthetic: ability to control bodily motions, an awareness of changes in momentum / balance / position, and the ability to handle objects with skill.

Musical: aptitude in the performance, composition and appreciation of musical patterns.

Interpersonal: highly developed ability to understand the intentions, motivations and desires of other people.

Intrapersonal: the capacity to understand oneself, to appreciate one's feelings, fears and motivations.

Naturalistic: the ability to recognize, categorize and draw upon certain features of the environment.

Gardner suggests that existential and moral intelligence might also be worthy of inclusion.

For years, education systems have emphasized the development of logical and linguistic intelligence, and traditional IQ tests have focused on measuring these abilities.

But IQ tests are not able to assess or predict one's ability to learn, to assimilate new information or to solve new problems.

Gardner believes that the purpose of education "should be to develop intelligences and to help people reach vocational and avocational goals that are appropriate to their particular spectrum of intelligences."

So the point here related to your life passion is not how smart you are, but how are you smart? What are your natural cognitive abilities, and how can you make the best use of them? When you play to your strengths, rather than struggling against pursuits that aren't natural for you, you provide fertile ground for passionate living.

Weekly Action

Do some reading on Gardner's multiple intelligence theory and the eight abilities he defines. Take one of the free online multiple intelligence tests like this one:

http://www.literacyworks.org/mi/assessment/findyourstrengths.html

How are you intelligent? Are you taking advantage of your natural strengths and abilities in your work or lifestyle? What are you doing now that isn't in line with your intelligence type?

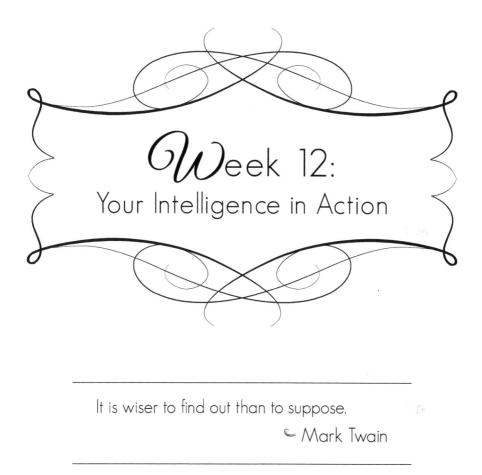

Week 12:
Your Intelligence in Action

It is wiser to find out than to suppose.

↳ Mark Twain

The theory of multiple intelligence is both good and bad. It's good because it eliminates the knee-jerk reaction of thinking we aren't capable or smart enough. It shows us exactly where we are most capable and naturally adept. But it's bad for the same reason.

Once we come to see *how* we are intelligent, we no longer have excuses for believing we're incapable. We can no longer fall back on *"I can't. I don't know how. I hate this. It's too hard for me."*

There is no reason to compare ourselves against the abilities and accomplishments of others. Now we are compelled to see ourselves as capable of achievement and happiness, a thought that is both exciting and daunting.

The theory of multiple intelligence teaches us two things about ourselves and our capacity for a passionate life.

First, it teaches us that we can choose to focus our time, energy and attention on pursuits that complement our natural abilities and interests. These could be interests and abilities you take for granted—ones you currently might not consider unique or remotely related to your intelligence.

Secondly, it reveals that when we must learn or perform outside of our natural cognitive abilities, we can use our particular intelligence type to approach learning and problems uniquely. There is almost always more than one way to undertake a task. We can choose to approach it in the way that is most natural for us, but that might not be the traditional or expected approach.

Rather than feeling like you are stuck in a boring or unfulfilling job, you can optimize your intelligence type and shift the way you approach your work or your role within your company.

You can find ways to strengthen your natural abilities through training, education or research—making yourself more viable in jobs where you will feel happy and comfortable.

Your intelligence type is another clue to your life passion. When you recognize and optimize your natural aptitudes, you place yourself on the path of least resistance. This shift will create more energy to put toward pinpointing precisely what makes you come alive with passion.

Now that you know your intelligence type, how can you optimize that in your life now? Think about ways you can align your natural cognitive abilities with your work, your hobbies and your lifestyle.

How can you strengthen your intelligence type or learn additional skills that support your type? As you begin to see where you are naturally intelligent, notice where you begin to feel excited or enthusiastic as you reflect on your cognitive abilities.

Week 13:
The Power of Creativity

If you hear a voice within you say, '*You cannot paint*,' then by all means paint, and that voice will be silenced.

⤷ Vincent Van Gogh

Do you consider yourself creative? If you work or play in one of the commonly accepted creative domains like the arts, writing, design, etc., you would likely answer yes. But accountants, lawyers, plumbers and others outside of these domains generally don't view themselves as creative types.

Many people believe that creativity is available only to those who are born with it. But this notion is just one of the myths about creativity. The truth is, everyone is creative—or has the capacity to be if they understand how creativity works in practice. You can be creative in any domain as long as it involves your intelligence.

Creativity is not a fixed ability, available to some lucky few but not to others. Creativity can be learned and applied to whatever you are doing. And the vehicle for creativity is imagination. Imagination allows us to step beyond our immediate sensory environment and envision something new in our minds eye. We can pull together all we have learned and experienced in the past, and use it to reframe our vision of the future in new and unique ways.

In his 2005 commencement speech at Stanford University, Steve Jobs, the creative genius behind Apple Computers, illustrates this with an example from his own life:

> *Much of what I stumbled into by following my curiosity and intuition turned out to be priceless later on. Let me give you one example: Reed College at that time offered perhaps the best calligraphy instruction in the country. Throughout the campus every poster, every label on every drawer was beautifully hand calligraphed. Because I had dropped out and didn't have to take the normal classes, I decided to take a calligraphy class to learn how to do this. I learned about serif and sans-serif and typefaces, about varying the space between different letter combinations, about what makes great typography great. It was beautiful, historical, artistically subtle in a way that science can't capture, and I found it fascinating. None of this had any hope of a practical application in my life. But ten years later, when we were designing the first Macintosh computer, it all came back to me, and we designed it all into*

the Mac. It was the first computer with beautiful typography. If I had not dropped into that single course in college, the Mac would never have had multiple typefaces or proportionally spaced fonts, and since Windows just copied the Mac, it's likely that no personal computer would have them.

But imagination alone isn't the same as creativity. Creativity takes imagination and puts it into action. It takes the vision you've formulated in your mind and applies it to something in the real world.

This applied imagination can work in any domain—from science, business, sports, math, and so on. Because we are so diverse in our intelligence, we have the ability to be creative in so many different ways. The creative process begins with an inkling, the seed of an idea or inspiration. The idea begins to roll around in your head, as you imagine various possibilities, options and outcomes.

As ideas formulate, you might test or practice some of them in the real world, putting them into action to judge what works or feels best. For an artist, that might mean doing a few sketches. For a scientist, it might mean jotting down some insights on a napkin and later testing them in a lab.

The process of generating ideas and then evaluating and refining them is central to the creative process regardless of the discipline or domain. Sometimes these ideas must sit with you for a while, allowing the subconscious to do its work in assimilating and processing information before an idea can come to life.

The creative process also involves tapping into your skills and abilities, using them in unique applications to form something original.

Creative inspiration often arises in seeing connections or similarities between things that you might not have noticed previously. It involves moving away from the linear and logical thinking you may have learned growing up so that you can see things from a fresh perspective. This is often referred to as "out-of-the-box" thinking.

So how does the creative process apply to you and finding your life passion? When you embrace your capacity for creativity and begin to shift your world view away from only linear, logical thinking, you can reframe everything in your life. You can see possibilities, combinations and opportunities in everything. There will no longer be just one "right" way to do things, to believe or to operate in your world.

When you allow yourself to imagine, to test, to experiment—you are opening the door to a world of potential. All of this potential is the soup from which you can ladle various new options and ideas for a new business, the book you want to write or any other pursuit you've placed on the back burner. Think about that—your life passion could be just one mind shift away.

Weekly Action

How do you currently view your creative abilities? Write down the ways you have used your imagination and applied it in the real world, whether in your work or personal life. How have you been limiting yourself creatively? Where have you held on to one world view in which you might open your mind to a new vision or approach? Write these down as well.

Week 14:
Skills, Talents and Aptitudes

We are all born with natural aptitudes, innate abilities and talents that are a part of who we are and the type of intelligence that is dominant within us. We also have many skills we've learned along the way—skills that may or may not be "natural" for us, but through desire or demand, we have learned them to some level of proficiency.

Often our natural aptitudes and talents require years of learning, training and practice to become proficient. We can build upon our natural abilities to make the most of what we were born with, and then use them for a career or avocation. But sometimes we have these aptitudes within us, and sadly they are never fully recognized, developed or utilized.

When I was forty, I went through a phase during which I feared all of my creativity had been sapped. I was in the thick of child-rearing and running a home, with all that this time of life entails. Most of my time was spent driving kids to activities, volunteering at their schools, cleaning up messes and preparing meals throughout the day. Although it was rewarding watching my children grow and thrive, I had no outlet for self-expression or creativity. In fact, I thought I had no creativity.

Someone suggested I read the book, *The Artist's Way, A Spiritual Path to Higher Creativity,* by Julia Cameron. In the book, Julia suggests that to stimulate creativity, you should commit to a period of "reading deprivation," so you have no excuse to avoid doing something playful and creative. She even provides a list of ideas.

I wanted to find something from her list that was easily interruptible, as I had a three-year-old at the time and knew my down-time came in five to ten minute increments. I chose drawing.

At the time, I thought I had no artistic ability whatsoever—my competency level was in the stick figure range. The last time I had seriously attempted drawing was in elementary school using crayons.

Nevertheless, I picked up a number two pencil along with a piece of construction paper, and found a drawing of a bird that looked simple to execute.

I focused on copying the lines of the drawing exactly as I saw them, and tried not to worry about the outcome. I was just drawing something for fun.

Most five-year-olds could have created something similar or better than my bird drawing. But this little drawing gave me a sense of pride and a budding awareness.

I could draw something better than stick figures. I could look at lines and shading and reproduce something that remotely resembled the bird I was attempting to copy.

The best thing that resulted from this first attempt was that I made a second attempt, and then a third, and so on. After a few more attempts at animals and still-life, I realized I really enjoyed drawing faces. If I just focused on reproducing lines and shading, without worrying about the outcome, I could create something fairly decent.

A couple of months later (*with no art classes or any professional instruction*), I completed a drawing of my then three-year-old daughter that I did from a photo of her.

Eventually, with a little more practice (but still no art classes), I was able to loosen up a bit without having to reproduce faces exactly as I saw them, and I was drawing pencil portraits for other people at their request.

I'm not telling you this story to awe you with my artistic ability. I am far from being a professional artist and could certainly use a lot of real instruction and practice. I am sharing this experience with you to let you know that you have hidden talents and abilities—things bottled up inside of you that you may not know you are capable of.

When I discovered this drawing ability, I actually feared something might be wrong with me—like a brain tumor or the beginning of some mental illness.

I couldn't understand how I'd gone my entire life not being able to reproduce the simplest figure artistically, and within a couple of months, people were asking me to draw portraits of their children. Where did this come from?

What I know today is that this ability was always there, lying dormant within me. I'd never seriously tried drawing before, and any small attempt at it led me to believe I had no ability.

Once I tried and let go of expectations of judgment or outcomes, I was able to enjoy the process of just doing something creative. This enjoyment gave me the desire to practice and learn.

Not all of my creative attempts have resulted in success, but others have—like writing and blogging. With these two, I had no idea what I was getting into when I first started. I just knew the process was fun and fulfilling. Now I make a full-time living from this work. That wasn't my intention, but here I am.

We often take for granted or totally miss many of our natural abilities, believing they aren't anything unique or useful. We don't recognize them as a special talent or ability because we may (*falsely*) assume they are available or come easily to everyone.

For example, perhaps you are a good listener . . . or you know how to keep things organized . . . or you can keep a meeting on track. At first blush, these may not seem like unique and special talents.

But these abilities aren't naturally available to everyone. And they are abilities that can be developed into something more—something useful or even profitable.

Right now, you may be taking advantage of some of your natural aptitudes. You may be in a career that aligns with your intelligence type and abilities. You may have studied or trained to enhance your abilities and become an expert.

Or you may be working in a field that has little to do with your in-born aptitudes. Perhaps you were encouraged or coerced in that direction by well-meaning parents or mentors. Maybe you didn't know what to do when you started a career, so you took the first decent job that became available.

But whether or not you are utilizing your aptitudes, if you aren't feeling passionate in your work or your life, something is amiss. You aren't taking advantage of your natural aptitudes in a way that makes you come alive, that fosters enthusiasm and fulfillment.

The same holds true for your skills. You've learned many skills related to your natural abilities and talents. And you have other skills learned from necessity—hundreds of skills you don't even think about.

They have become habits you practice unconsciously or with little awareness of the effort it took you to achieve them over time. These might include the general tasks of daily living (*preparing meals, balancing a checkbook, cleaning the house, planting a garden*) or skills you've learned on jobs, volunteer activities, hobbies or projects.

Becoming fully conscious of these abilities is the first step in finding the combination of them that most excites us.

Using creativity to imagine new ways to apply and expand your skills and aptitudes will generate a larger pool of options for your potential life passion.

Weekly Action

Go back and read over the information on your intelligence type. Using that information, think about all of your natural aptitudes and talents—no matter how small or seemingly insignificant.

Start making a list of these and continue to work on it as additional thoughts come to mind. Next, begin making a similar list of all of your learned skills, even if they are not related to your natural abilities or your current career.

To help you remember your skills, you can find lists of skills online for both personal and professional life.

Week 15:
A Matter of Priorities

Once you do the exercise of writing down all of your natural abilities and skills, you might be surprised at how much you have accomplished over the years and how much you are capable of doing.

As adults, we forget to acknowledge these things within us. We forget how hard we've worked, and how much our brains have absorbed as we have grown and made lives for ourselves. None of your abilities should be ignored, even the most seemingly insignificant. They have served you well, and will continue to be beneficial to you and others throughout your life.

Most of us have a tendency to diminish ourselves. We compare our abilities and perceived level of success (*or lack thereof*) to others. We ignore our accomplishments and skills, only to focus with laser intensity on our flaws and failures. But on some level, we are all aware that we have more inside of us than we are using. That awareness creates a certain amount of tension, making us feel bad that we aren't living up to our potential.

Frankly, we can never live up to our fullest potential, because we have so many hidden and untapped abilities. That's not the point. The point is that you could be enjoying your life more fully than you are now.

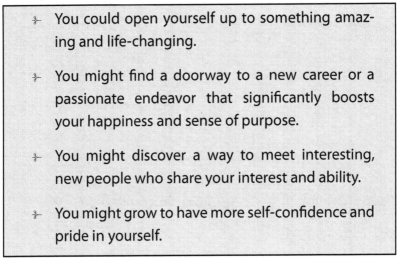

- You could open yourself up to something amazing and life-changing.

- You might find a doorway to a new career or a passionate endeavor that significantly boosts your happiness and sense of purpose.

- You might discover a way to meet interesting, new people who share your interest and ability.

- You might grow to have more self-confidence and pride in yourself.

At the very least, you could have an hour a day where you have fun, relax, try something new, disengage from TV or books and do something different.

Yes, you have untapped potential. But don't allow that knowledge to make you feel confused, fearful, or down on yourself. You have nothing to prove to anyone.

Look inside of yourself and pick something—anything—and give it a try. You never know where it might lead you!

In reality, you have enough skills and talents available to you *right now* to make a decent living, or create an exciting lifestyle, for the rest of your life.

And you have an endless capacity to learn new things, to become accomplished at new skills. There's enough information available online to learn virtually anything. And you can find endless information for pursuing or continuing your education if you desire—often with tuition-free or low-tuition options.

The problem isn't that you don't have the abilities, the skills or the opportunity to learn more and change your life. The problem is that there is so much available to you, it's hard to know where to start or how to make a change. It's hard to know which skills and abilities to focus on so you aren't spinning your wheels, investing your valuable time in the wrong direction.

Yes, you have many natural abilities, many skills and an abundance of opportunity to build on those. You have the intelligence and creativity to envision new ways of combining or utilizing your skills and aptitudes. But that doesn't mean you have to pursue or even enjoy all of those skills. In fact, you don't have the time to pursue all of them.

You can't do everything you are capable of doing in just one lifetime—but you can do *enough* of what you are capable of, and what you enjoy, to live a passionate and fulfilled life.

It's a matter of priorities. It's a matter of zeroing in on what is most interesting, most exciting and most fulfilling at any given time in your life and focusing your attention on that.

Weekly Action

Look at your list of natural abilities and your list of skills. Review the lists carefully, crossing through any abilities or skills that you don't really enjoy or know you don't wish to pursue in any significant way.

From your remaining lists, circle your top five natural abilities and your top five skills based on your level of enjoyment (*not necessarily your level of expertise*).

These can be skills and abilities where you might need additional training or education. Don't worry about that for now.

Week 16:
Cultivating Happiness

Many persons have a wrong idea of what
constitutes true happiness. It is not attained
through self-gratification but through fidel-
ity to a worthy purpose.

⌐ Helen Keller

"I just want to be happy." Isn't that the mantra we've all repeated to ourselves at various times through the years?

By its very definition, a passionate life equates to a general sense of happiness and well-being.

Happiness often appears elusive and random. We know it will

appear at certain times—when we fall in love, when we have a big success, when we are on vacation, when things are going our way.

But *sustained happiness* is another matter.

Life circumstances can undermine our happiness. Our moods and health can diminish our joy and contentment. Other people can say or do things to evaporate our happy mood. Often these things are out of our control.

Even when things appear to be going well, there are times when we just don't feel happy.

We are restless, bored, uninspired, frustrated, unmotivated, stressed, overwhelmed or off-balance. And it's hard to pinpoint exactly why we feel this way or how to shift back to feeling joyful and happy.

In fact, sometimes we spend more time feeling unhappy than happy. Wouldn't it be great to figure out how to feel happy 60, 70, 80 or even 90 percent of the time? Is that possible?

Let's start by looking at what creates happiness.

Part of our happiness levels are determined by genetics—50 percent in fact, according to psychologist and happiness researcher, Dr. Sonja Lyubomirsky. Some of us are more predisposed to being naturally happy than others. This is our happiness "set point."

But here's the surprising statistic. Only 10 percent of our happiness levels result from our life circumstances—our lifestyle, finances, appearance, etc. This is a stunningly small percentage considering how much time we spend pursuing happiness through these circumstances! It appears we have things backward.

There is a diminishing point of return with happiness and life circumstances. Once we have our basic needs met and a handful of our wants, attaining better life circumstances doesn't measurably improve happiness.

So after genetics and life circumstances, 40 percent of our happiness levels are in our control. It's a significant percentage that can impact our lives for the better.

In her book, *The How of Happiness: A New Approach to Getting the Life You Want*, Dr. Lyubomirsky reveals the data from her years of research on what fosters happiness—at least in that controllable 40 percent area. She discovered twelve strategies that are proven to increase happiness if practiced habitually. These include:

- Regularly expressing gratitude
- Cultivating an optimistic outlook
- Reducing over-thinking and social comparisons
- Practicing acts of kindness
- Nurturing relationships
- Practicing engaging activities
- Remembering and savoring life's joys
- Committing to goals

   ✢   Learning to forgive

   ✢   Practicing religion or spirituality

   ✢   Taking care of your body

Living a life of passion requires finding a way to implement these strategies every day. Even as you are on the search for your life passion, you can substantially increase your levels of happiness right now by practicing these actions on a regular basis.

You don't need to wait for your circumstances to change in order to find happiness in your current life.

If you begin your passion search from a position of happiness, then finding your passion will only make your life more amazing. And who knows, perhaps your life passion will emerge from one of these happiness-generating actions.

Weekly Action

Look at the list of Dr. Lyubomirsky's twelve strategies for increasing happiness. What are you doing now on this list that makes you happy? What strategies require more attention from you? Select one or two of these strategies to focus on during the week, and pay attention to how they make you feel when you practice them.

Week 17:
Finding Joy, Fun and Fulfillment

One of Dr. Lyubomirsky's strategies for happiness is remembering and savoring life's joys. Just the act of conjuring up past events that were joyful and replaying them in your mind is enough to give you a surge of happy feelings.

Most of us don't spend a lot of time daydreaming about past events or circumstances that made us happy. If we do think about the past, it's often with remorse, anger or regret. Usually, we are quite busy dealing with the issues at hand or worrying about the future.

If the issues at hand are happy and fulfilling, by all means, stay in the present moment and savor it fully. However, when you are unhappy, bored, worried, stressed or confused—reflecting on joyful past events is a great way to shift your state of mind.

But there's another important benefit to reflecting on past joys in relation to your life passion work. Reflection can remind you of past activities, work, hobbies and childhood dreams that once put you in that happy, passionate state of mind—the state you want to attain for the rest of your life. It can provide clues to what you want more of in your life and inspire you to make room for those things.

Randy Pausch, the computer science professor at Carnegie Mellon University who died in 2008 of pancreatic cancer, knew firsthand the power and potential of connecting with past dreams and joys.

In his famous speech (*and book*), *The Last Lecture*, Pausch talks about "really achieving your childhood dreams." Pausch wanted to be a Disney Imagineer and build theme park attractions ever since visiting Disneyland when he was eight years old. Unfortunately, when he graduated with his Ph.D., he was soundly rejected by Disney and moved on in his academic career. *"So that was a bit of a setback,"* he said. *"But remember, the brick walls are there for a reason. The brick walls are not there to keep us out. The brick walls are there to give us a chance to show how badly we want something."*

The joy and passion Randy felt during his Disneyland trip never left him. It inspired him in his work as a professor of computer-human interaction at Carnegie Mellon. Many years later, Randy Pausch was able to fulfill his dream.

Over the years, he became a famous virtual reality researcher, and when he heard about Disney's Aladdin magic carpet ride, he convinced both Disney and the University to allow him to work on the project. He then continued as a consultant for Disney during his tenure at Carnegie Mellon.

He didn't assume that his initial rejection from Disney meant the end of his childhood dream. He found other outlets for his dream, and later came back to it when the time was right. Reflecting on past joys and passions, even those that never materialized, will keep you connected to the energy and positivity that these memories foster.

When you look back over your life and your work, you may see patterns emerge of activities, hobbies, projects, endeavors, trips, relationships and interactions that were joyful, fun or fulfilling. And perhaps the timing is ripe now for your past joys to materialize into a life passion. At the very least, you want to find a way to allow more joyful activities and relationships into your life.

Weekly Action

Create two lists—one titled "personal life" and the other "professional life." Think back over events and circumstances in each area of your life in which you experienced joy, fun or fulfillment (*or even all three*). When have you felt "in the flow?" Get as specific as possible. Dig deep to discern what aspect of the event or situation fostered the good feeling.

Circle any that were truly profound and important for you—that you would like to see as part of your life right now.

Week 18:
House Cleaning

Remembering happy and fulfilling past events can be an inspiring exercise. It awakens you from the weariness and monotony of your present circumstances. It reminds you there were times, however brief, when you felt enthusiastic and fully-engaged in life.

Perhaps you can recreate these events. Perhaps you can explore them more fully.

So your brain starts firing up. You begin to envision new possibilities. You are reminded of your past dreams for a career, a certain lifestyle or a pursuit you neglected long ago. Maybe, just maybe, this is the time to try again. This is the time to start over.

But then a nagging little anxiety sets in. A sense of defeat settles over you like a dark cloud before your fledgling enthusiasm has a chance to take hold. How can you attempt anything else right now?

Your life is already busy and complicated. Your schedule is maxed out. Now you realize why you let those memories settle to the recesses of your mind. Why conjure them up when you have no time to do anything about them?

No time. Too busy. But let's be honest—this is just a story we tell ourselves.

This busyness is a state we create for ourselves when we have a void. We fill time when we don't have anything better to do. We fill time so we don't feel empty or useless.

And when we haven't found our passion, when we aren't sure what will make us happy, we fill time with work, tasks and projects that don't inspire or excite us. In fact, we might even despise these time-fillers. But we do them anyway because doing nothing feels worse.

We also fill time because we are afraid. We are afraid if we create space, we'll actually have to take action on our dreams. We'll have to experiment and make ourselves vulnerable to something unproven, something which might make us look bad or feel worse than we already do.

What if I fail? What if I'm not capable? What if it's all a waste of time? So we use time-fillers as an excuse to avoid trying.

But let's take a hard look at those time-fillers. Aren't they really time wasters? You are wasting your precious (*and finite*) time on this

Earth doing things that aren't meaningful to you—maybe even things you hate. Is that really what you want? Ask your higher self, the part of you that so deeply wants a passionate life. Is that really what your want for your beautiful life? If you had one day left to live, would mindless activities and boring work be part of your day?

Weekly Action

This week, mentally go through every hour of your day, every day of the week. Make notes about how you are spending your time. Look at all of your activities, tasks, projects and down-time.

Review the way you spend time on your job. How much TV do you watch? How much time do you spend surfing the net? How much time are you in your car? Which of these actions are just time-fillers? Which do you actually hate?

If you let go of these, how much time could you gain? Are you willing to let go?

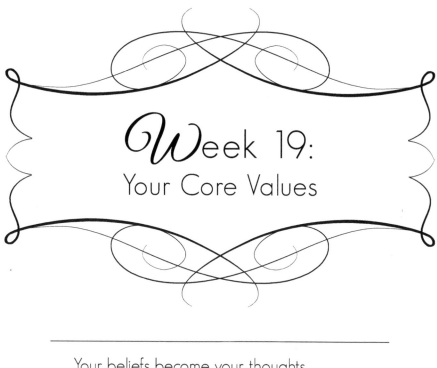

Week 19:
Your Core Values

Your beliefs become your thoughts,
Your thoughts become your words,
Your words become your actions,
Your actions become your habits,
Your habits become your values,
Your values become your destiny.

— Mahatma Gandhi

There are times in life when we feel lost. Something seems off, but we can't put our finger on it. We just know that nothing feels exciting or interesting anymore. Happiness and peace of mind have abandoned us. We are paddling along with our heads just above water—aimlessly, sometimes hopelessly.

When this happens, one common response is to push harder. You put on a great game face and assure yourself this will pass. "If I just ignore it then it will go away." Sometimes it does go away—briefly. You fill your life with activities and distractions, and maybe you feel better for a while. But in quiet moments, the emptiness creeps back in.

Another reaction is struggle and despair. That lost feeling makes you claw around like a drowning man, grasping at salvation wherever you can find it.

You ask friends, go to counseling, read self-help books, attempting this or that method for happiness, peace of mind, and for the elusive "thing" that will provide them. When nothing seems to "work," you sink deeper into despair.

The strange thing about happiness and peace of mind is that they are ephemeral. You finally think you have found them, and then after a few months or years, they float away inexplicably. And you're left stunned, because you really thought you had it right this time.

The wonderful and terrible thing about the human psyche is that it is constantly changing.

We silently (or sometimes tumultuously) drift into a new phase of life, but no one tells us to expect upheaval. Or if they do, we don't believe them because we have our particular life under complete control. And then it happens. You step into the shifting sands of a life transition and you are stuck. The more your flail, the more stuck you become. It is totally unexpected and frightening.

But all of that flailing isn't a complete waste. It can be a cue that this is the time to reevaluate. This is the time to accept that everything you once valued as most important may not be what you value now. (*Did you notice that the word "reevaluate" has the word "value" in it?*)

Your values have changed over time, maybe imperceptibly at first, but then your restlessness, boredom or depression are your psyche's way of yelling "Pay attention!"

So what are values? In short, they are what is most important to you—your principles, your standards, the basis for your conscience and integrity.

Each one of us has hundreds of values, but very few of us can define what they are or which ones are the guiding values in our lives. Without that clarity, it is easy to disconnect with what is truly important to you and allow your life to slip out of alignment with your values.

When you're in the midst of a life transition and searching for your passion, it's essential to take stock of your current values, recognize where they have changed, and then do whatever you can to align your life with these values. Why?

Because living in harmony with your most important values—your core values—creates the fertile environment for finding your life passion and feeling content and balanced. Some people call this living authentically. Your core values serve as a measuring stick for all of your choices and decisions, keeping you in line with the person you want to be and the life you wish to lead.

When you do the exercise of reassessing your core values, you help yourself in two ways. First, the desperate flailing stops because you gain a sense of control over your destiny. Secondly, you discover that you always have access to the answers for yourself if you take the time and space to search for them. You will save yourself a lot of time and angst if you begin inside with your values instead of trying to randomly change things outside of you.

Weekly Action

Think about your most important life values and begin writing down value words that represent these. They could include values like freedom, love, flexibility, creativity, order, peace, leadership, etc.

Write down as many possible values as you can think of, then circle five that are most important in your personal life and five that are most important in your professional life.

Are your life and work currently centered on these values?

Week 20:
The Purpose of Purpose

When you are struggling to find your life passion, it's easy to be consumed by feelings of confusion, even when you have defined your values.

You might look at people born with one or more life passions and envy their laser-like enthusiasm as they pursue their calling. How did they figure it out? What were they born with that you don't have?

The path toward uncovering a life passion is often long and circuitous. It can be a journey without a road map, a maze of false starts and abandoned pursuits. But it doesn't have to be this way.

When you have a purpose directing you that incorporates your values, you've created a framework for finding your life passion. A life purpose can be the benchmark for discovering pursuits that light the fire of your passion.

Scott Harrison's story is a perfect example.

Scott was a strikingly handsome eighteen-year-old when he set out for New York City with dreams of fame and fortune. And it didn't take long for him to make his dream a reality.

He quickly got involved in the nightclub scene, and within a few years became a top promoter of nightclubs and fashion events. He was making lots of money, traveling the world and enjoying an extravagant life of excess. He was living the dream.

But at the age of twenty-eight, he realized something had to change. He was living selfishly and arrogantly, feeling morally and emotionally bankrupt. His high-rolling life felt meaningless.

So he asked himself the question, "*What would the opposite of my life look like?*" He decided to take a year off to pursue something that had no resemblance to his life in New York.

He signed up for volunteer service as a photojournalist aboard a floating hospital with a group called Mercy Ships, a humanitarian organization which offers free medical care in the world's poorest nations.

In Liberia, Scott spent time photographing in many remote villages, including a leper colony. "*I put a face to the world's 1.2 billion living in poverty—those living on less than $365 a year—money I used to blow on a bottle of Grey Goose vodka at a fancy club,*" says Scott.

He focused his energy on bringing clean water to these people—a scarcity in most developing countries. Often the only source of water is a polluted swamp.

Over time, Scott saw this as his mission—his purpose in life. He became passionate about finding ways to create clean water sources for the over 800 million people living without them.

He founded Charity Water (charitywater.org), a hugely successful non-profit organization bringing clean, safe drinking water to people in developing countries.

Some of the same people he used to party with are now donating their time and resources to Scott's passion.

For years, Scott was living without a purpose, and for a time he was enjoying himself.

But eventually he came to realize his life was meaningless and empty.

He recommitted to his personal values and through his emptiness found a way to connect his life and work to something larger and more meaningful – something that allows him to leave a positive legacy. He understands his purpose and has built a passionate career around it.

Is having a life purpose essential in order to find your passion? Not necessarily. But a purpose infuses your life with something we all deeply long for—meaning.

At the end of the day, we want to feel our time on Earth has made a difference. When you are doing something you love, something that makes a difference in the world, passion is inevitable.

Weekly Action

Think about your life right now. Write down all of the ways, even the most insignificant, that you are making a difference and doing something meaningful.

Do any of these stand-out as something that might be your life purpose?

Think about people whose lives seem purposeful to you. What are they doing that inspires you? What is deeply meaningful to you? What kind of legacy do you want to leave on the world?

Week 21:
A Beautiful Vision

Defining your core values and sketching out a life purpose can create momentum and clarity in your search for a life passion. Now you have parameters. Now you have benchmarks. Is this pursuit in line with my values? Does this activity further my life purpose?

You can begin narrowing the field of options and ideas. If one of your values is "family," and you are spending twelve hours a day on your job, are you really living in line with this core value? If your life purpose is to be a peacemaker, but you are constantly arguing with your spouse, are you moving yourself closer to that purpose?

You see, life passion begins in the minutiae of your life and extends into the small and large choices you make for yourself every day.

Every corner of your life needs to be addressed and tidied up so that you have the emotional integrity and energy to find your true passion. Every aspect should be measured against your values and purpose. If you are unsure about your life purpose, then simply use your values as a guide.

The best way to get your "life house" in order is to create a vision of how you want it to look. Successful athletes visualize their goals before they perform. Successful businesses have a vision for the future of their company.

Having a vision for your own life allows you to "see" all aspects of your life at the highest level you wish to achieve. It allows you to picture yourself as the "who you want to be" beyond who you are right now.

Having a vision also sets intention. It tricks the mind into believing that something already exists and you are working toward it. The person you want to be, and the life you want to live, is there in your imagination. Now you just need to connect the dots and push the power button to bring this vision to life.

A life vision can be created for one year or several years, but no more than five. As you know, we continue to change and evolve over time, and your core values and vision should evolve with you. Creating a vision is an exercise you should repeat several times over your lifetime.

What should a life vision include? Everything. Everything that constitutes the elements of your life: work, relationships, finances, lifestyle, hobbies, spiritual life, family, community, home, children, friends, education and personal growth. Each of these areas should be carefully defined and regularly refined—within the framework of your core values and life purpose.

Most businesses have a vision statement. One of the best I've seen is that of Kraft Foods. Kraft has crafted a statement that clearly reflects their values and purpose:

Our Vision...
Helping People Around the World Eat and Live Better

Our vision captures the essence of who we are. Everything we do flows from our vision. We just don't happen to be a business that sells food—it's what we're all about. Our vision is about meeting consumers' needs and making food an easier, healthier, more enjoyable part of life.

Our vision tells the world—our employees, customers, consumers and the communities where we make and sell our products—what we care about. It captures the importance of health and wellness, but it also embodies all the ways we can eat and live better, such as the enjoyment of a dessert, the convenience of a microwave meal, the safety and value of our products and the services and solutions we provide.

View each of your life areas (*work, relationships, money, etc.*) as an individual "business." Each of your businesses is integrated by a shared purpose and set of values. Using those as a framework, you can create a vision statement for each of your "life businesses," reflecting the same attitude of seriousness and determination that Kraft Foods and others have for the future of their companies.

You may not have a clear, definitive or complete outline of your vision for each area of your life right now, but you will likely have a general vision. You will have rough sketch of how you want your relationships to feel, how you want to be involved in your community, how you will make and manage money, etc. Your vision can be written or in the form of a vision board.

A life vision is the character study of the person you want to become, based on your values and life purpose. It is more an impressionist painting than a photograph. But it will serve as a beacon, guiding you closer to your life passion and motivating you on your search.

Weekly Action

Review your core values and life purpose. Keep them handy as you work on this action. Begin with one area of your life from those listed above or any others that might be important to you. Then write a vision statement and a few paragraphs about your ideal self and circumstances in that area of your life. You can be very specific or just write a rough outline.

If you prefer, you can create a vision board rather than writing out your vision. A vision board is a poster board or cork board on which you glue or pin images that reflect your life vision. To get ideas and inspiration for either a vision statement or vision board, go online to research samples of each.

Week 22:
The Power of Process

The road of life twists and turns and no two directions are ever the same. Yet our lessons come from the journey, not the destination.

℃ Don Williams, Jr.

All you want to do is find your life passion, but suddenly the contents of your life have been upended and are scattered all over the floor. Your personality, intelligence, creativity, joys, aptitudes, values, purpose and vision have been pulled apart, dissected and rearranged.

Twenty-two weeks in, and you're no closer to your life passion than you were during week one. Maybe it feels that way, but you are closer—much closer—even if it seems like a big mess right now.

When you clean out your closet, you end up with stuff all over the floor . . . piles to discard, piles to recycle, piles to sort and put away. At first, things are in more disarray than when you started. You feel completely overwhelmed and wonder why you started this stupid project in the first place.

But as you slowly sort through everything, you see what is important to you. You see the value of simplifying, prioritizing and organizing.

You begin to enjoy the process because you have a vision of the outcome. You're not exactly sure how it's all going to look, but you can see things taking shape.

The process of any project—including the search for your life passion—shouldn't be a means to an end.

All of the steps toward uncovering your passion aren't just steps. They are clues. These clues include valuable information that you are collecting and sorting through to refine your life priorities and define who you want to be.

The process itself provides dozens of small outcomes, various finish lines that shift your perspective, open your eyes, challenge your way of seeing yourself and the possibilities before you.

So here's one more mind shift for you: shift the way you perceive the process of discovering your life passion. Enjoy each exercise, each discovery about yourself, and the clarity you are gaining about who you are and how you want to live your life.

Not many people take the time to do this important work. Not many people are willing to put all the contents of their lives on to the floor and sort through them. But you are. And that should be both acknowledged and celebrated.

Remember, doing this work means you are taking control of your life and creating your future. You alone are making the important decisions about the next phase of your life.

That is empowering. You don't need to feel hopeless or helpless or stuck or bored or confused. Look at you—you are doing this important work. You are making things happen in your life. Enjoy the process.

Weekly Action

Go back and review the work you have done over the past twenty-two weeks. Look at each of the actions and what you have discovered about yourself. See if there are areas you might want to refine.

Look at all of the information with an eye for patterns, recurring themes, or places that stir an ember of enthusiasm. Make note of these and acknowledge your work so far.

Week 23:
Getting Support

Being heard is so close to being loved that
for the average person, they are almost
indistinguishable.

‿ David Augsburger

So here you are standing at a crossroads between your old life and
the life you are beginning to envision for your future. Maybe that
new life isn't clear just yet. But perhaps some ideas are simmering. Maybe you are feeling a spark of enthusiasm about some

possibility—a thread of an idea that if pulled could lead you to amazing places.

You've been operating under the radar screen up until now. This is a highly personal process—cracking yourself open and digging around inside.

Finding your passion involves more than just having your dream life land on top of you unexpectedly. You have to get your hands dirty. You have to get fiercely real with yourself.

While you are digging around in your own internal world, do you really want someone else peering over your shoulder and making comments and suggestions?

Spouses, family members and friends may have the best intentions with their ideas or input, but in the early stages of your passion search, you need a clear head free from distractions, negativity or confusion.

Sometimes our loved ones feel threatened by the possibility of change—even positive change. If you appear to be rocking the boat and making waves in the nice, secure and predictable life you have together, it's bound to cause concern or outright rebellion.

Even if your passion pursuit makes no impact whatsoever on your loved one's life, simply making a positive move for yourself can stir the emotional pot for them, causing feelings of fear and insecurity. This is especially true with your spouse or life partner.

Of course, you can't keep this passion work to yourself forever.

In fact, you shouldn't keep it to yourself. The time comes when you need to come clean and share. Why? Because you need a safe and supportive environment for your fledging passion to take root and grow.

You need the support and blessing of those closest to you in order to feel confident about learning, experimenting and ultimately making the life changes that your passion might require. And healthy relationships demand that you involve those whose lives are intertwined with yours. It's the right thing to do.

But it is up to you to set the stage for that safe and supportive environment. Once you feel the timing is right, you need to foster the buy-in and support of those who may be affected by what you are doing—most commonly your spouse or partner.

Even if your loved one has been on board since the beginning of your passion work, the changes occurring inside of you will have a ripple effect. It's up to you to assure and inform them you are doing this work mindfully, responsibly and with their best interest in mind—as well as your own.

The best way to do this is through regular, open communication in which you ask for the kind of support you need. In these early stages of exploration, that support may be patience and listening. Later on, it may require that you work together to figure out how to alter or manage your lives to accommodate your new passion.

If you don't communicate regularly about your passion ideas and plans, your loved one may feel threatened or resentful, and could subtly or overtly sabotage your plans. But with regular

communication, you can navigate potential emotional and practical land mines together. Yes, it may involve some compromise for
both of you, but living a passionate life and having loving relationships shouldn't be mutually exclusive.

Weekly Action

Whose support and blessing do you most need
during this passion work? How have you communicated with them so far, and what has been the
response or reaction?

Plan a meeting with your loved one to begin or
further the conversation about your life passion
work. Reassure them if necessary.

Ask for their ideas if needed. Tell them specifically
how they can support you as your work toward your
passion.

Week 24:
Attitude is Everything

Your living is determined not so much by what life brings to you as by the attitude you bring to life; not so much by what happens to you as by the way your mind looks at what happens.

≗ Khalil Gibran

Finding your passion involves detective work to learn more about your personality, motivations, values and skills. It also requires the careful prioritizing and integration of these elements.

Your passion is ultimately uncovered where those most important elements intersect with your willingness to take bold action, even when you may feel uncertain. Ultimately, it requires a leap of faith.

What is it that allows you to take that leap? It all boils down to a positive attitude. Call it self-confidence or fearlessness or courage. But really, it's simply a choice you make to gather information, take action and believe that things will work out. And most importantly, you must choose to believe in yourself during this time of change.

In May of 1943, Olympic distance runner Louis Zamperini was a Second Lieutenant in the Army Air Forces, serving as a bombardier. Along with his pilot Phil Phillips, tail-gunner Mac MacNamara and several other crewmen, Louis was assigned to go on a search and rescue mission in a B-52 known to have mechanical difficulties.

Not long after take-off, the plane crashed into the ocean 850 miles west of Oahu, killing eight of the eleven men aboard. Louis, Phil and Mac survived, living on a small raft with no food or water, subsisting on rainwater, birds and small fish. Through their ordeal, they fought off daily shark attacks, storms that nearly capsized their boat and air attacks from a Japanese bomber.

From the beginning, Mac was despondent and hopeless. He felt they were doomed and sank into periods of lethargy and despair. Although Louis and Phil knew there was good reason to share in Mac's despair, they were determined to keep thoughts of death and hopelessness out of their minds.

They spent their long hours playing mental games, challenging each other and attempting to calculate their position and distance to land. They devised tools for catching rainwater, creating a shelter from a deflated raft, and fashioning fish hooks from bird bones. They acted "as if" they were going to survive.

On the thirty-third day at sea, Mac—who had wasted away both physically and emotionally—died on the raft. Louis and Phil survived, living on the raft for a total of forty-seven days until they reached land, where they were promptly captured by Japanese soldiers. After their ordeal on the raft, they spent nearly three years in POW camps before they were finally freed. They both went on to marry, have children and live successful lives. Louis Zamperini's story of resilience, survival and forgiveness is the subject of the bestselling book *Unbroken*, by Laura Hillenbrand. As of this writing, Louis is now ninety-five years old and still active and engaged in life.

Of course, Louis' story is an extreme example. But it illustrates the power of mental attitude. People who are survivors, who are successful, who are passionate—aren't just lucky. They are actively in touch with their outlook and moods. And they proactively make the effort to turn themselves around when they start to feel despair, low confidence, fear or uncertainty.

According to psychologist Richard Wiseman, author of *The Luck Factor*, people who appear to be lucky share similar attitudes and behaviors.

> ⚹ They maximize and act upon chance opportunities (*taking a leap of faith*).
>
> ⚹ They follow their intuition and promote their intuitive abilities through meditation or other means.

> ⨟ They have an expectation of positive outcomes and success. They act "as if."
>
> ⨟ And finally, they are able to reframe a "bad" situation and turn it into something positive.

In the pursuit to uncover your life passion, attitude can make the difference between seeing an opportunity or missing the boat; between finding something to learn from failure or giving up as a result. Positive attitude creates a magnet that attracts you to what you love, and attracts the right people and opportunities to you to help you make it a reality. In this life passion work, attitude is everything.

Weekly Action

Set aside fifteen minutes this week to assess your attitude around your life passion work. Are you feeling positive and hopeful, or do you feel yourself sinking with doubts and frustration? Refer back to your vision, and create a mental picture of yourself living that vision. Let this mental exercise foster excitement and hope around the real possibility of a new life.

When you catch yourself sinking into negativity, reframe your thinking to positive thoughts or distract yourself with something engaging until the feelings pass. What else can you do this week to create or sustain a positive attitude about your future?

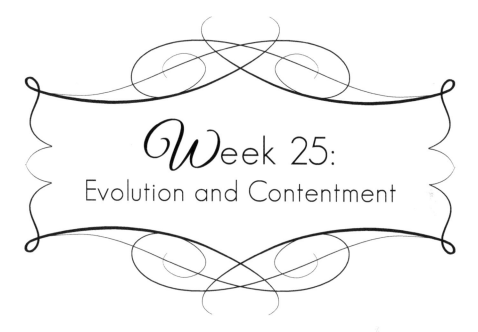

Week 25:
Evolution and Contentment

Is it possible to want to change your life, to seek your passion, but still be happy with your life right now? Can you be content and evolving at the same time?

I firmly believe it is both possible and imperative. Creating this powerful balance between happiness in the moment and action toward a more passionate life is something we should strive for every day.

Leo Babauta, creator of the blog *Zen Habits*, writes regularly about contentedness. He suggests you don't need to wait for change—for something better, for the future—before you are content. You can be content right now if you choose to see all of the good and beauty around you in the present moment.

Truthfully, the present moment is our only reality. The past and future don't exist. So if right now is spent longing for some vision of the future, we aren't truly living and savoring the blessings of right now.

Longing and struggling against "what is" causes suffering. Wishing for more, for something different, for something better at the expense of contentment in the moment robs us of life.

So why should you focus on your vision of a passionate life if it pulls you away from the moment?

Well here's a secret: change and transformation will happen to you whether or not you define how it will happen. Change is a constant of life.

But you have to power to define how that change will happen. You can be the *creator* of your life rather than a reactor to it. Can one be a life passion creator and content in the moment all at the same time?

How do you become the best version of yourself while loving yourself just as you are? Begin with the mind shift that both are possible.

When you accept this truth, you reduce the tension between thinking you should be content right now and the inner urging for something more. There is a way to create a balance.

View *the process* of personal evolution as place for happiness and contentment. Rather than holding back happiness while you await an outcome, enjoy every step along the path. Every revelation, every small action toward your passion, should be savored and celebrated. Life is a process.

During the process, you will experience tedious, boring or even painful moments. Rather than resisting or struggling against these times, breathe into them. Even see the beauty in them. Shift your thinking so you become aware of even the smallest value these moments add to your experience of life.

An action imbued with purpose and meaning becomes a ritual. Each action step along the way to your life passion is a microcosm of the outcome you are seeking.

Rather than viewing each step as a boring task, turn it into a ritual— a crystalline droplet of your beautiful vision for yourself.

And remember, failure is part of process. Even though failure stings, the venom it injects actually serves our growth. Failure means you are engaged in life because you've taken a risk toward your life passion. Evolve your thinking about failure. Learn to embrace it.

Whatever you are doing during your life passion journey, focus on it. Savor it. Roll around in it. Love it even if it is painful. Don't struggle against or wish for something more. If you are doing it now, it is the most important thing in the world.

Have a beginner's mindset in all things. Accept that even if you are an expert, there is always more to learn. You can learn from the humblest among us. You can learn new ways of thinking. You can learn to appreciate many points of view. Stay open to all possibilities with eager expectation.

Be content with being the best self you can be in each moment—
because you will always be in the process of becoming. Make each
moment your passion destination until you find your passion.

Weekly Action

As you work toward your life passion, how are you
living the rest of your life? Is your focus so much on
the possibility of passion that you are ignoring the
moment?

Think of ways you can imbue every moment with
passion and focus creatively on the task at hand.

Create rituals around your passion work by setting
aside special time for reading and reflection. Create
a peaceful space in your house where you do this
work, and mentally bless the actions you are taking
every week.

Week 26:
Maximizing Mentors

Tell me and I forget, teach me and I may
remember, involve me and I learn.

                  ~ Benjamin Franklin

When I was in the throes of my own life passion work, I participated in an endless variety of courses and workshops, hoping they might guide me toward "that thing" I was so desperately seeking.

My friends Larry and Jody were offering a workshop called "Life Compass," helping participants find the life they were meant to live. I signed up for it, not realizing it would give me exposure to a side of them I hadn't known before.

I'd interacted with Larry and Jody for years through our children. Our daughters trained together as ballet dancers, and Jody and I had spent time together in carpools, recitals and waiting around at dance studios.

I got to know Larry a bit later. I started hearing bits and pieces of a new venture he'd started—something about coaching people to align their lives with their spiritual goals.

As I was thinking about life coaching for myself, I talked with Larry to learn more about his work and to take their Life Compass workshop. In the process, I learned the most incredible thing about them.

Larry had worked for years in an executive job with a prestigious corporation. He and Jody lived in a big house in a gated community. One day Larry came home from work and announced to Jody that he'd experienced a spiritual transformation. He'd been inspired to quit his job and start a non-profit working with people on spiritual awakening. *"Oh, and by the way honey, we'll need to sell the house to do this."*

He neglected that "communicate early and often" rule. Needless to say, this turn of events did a number on their marriage. This person was not the Larry whom Jody had married.

But here's the amazing part. Larry had discovered his life passion. He couldn't walk away from it in spite of fears about his marriage, finances and a myriad of other concerns about starting a new venture.

And as Larry aligned with his authentic self, incredibly Jody did too.

Together, they found a way to share this dream and make it real. Larry started Cloud Walk, a non-profit organization dedicated to serving others in their spiritual growth.

They regularly conduct workshops and retreats and have touched hundreds of lives. It continues to grow, and Larry is clearly where he should be.

The Cloud Walk offices are in a wonderful, light-filled cottage which he shares with Jody. Along the way, Jody has found her own passion and started a retail business called The Garden Within.

Part of the cottage is her retail space where she sells unique, locally-made jewelry, clothing, art and garden goodies. She also works with Larry at Cloud Walk on workshops and retreats.

So now this husband and wife have each found where they are supposed to be. Their contentment is palpable. They are in this great space together, working with people who want to grow spiritually.

Jody and Larry don't know it, but they were my early mentors in my own life passion work. They taught me the power of life passion and its inherent value over material things.

They reinforced that it is possible to overcome serious obstacles and still make passion a reality. And they revealed through their daily lives and work that it is possible to be happy and fulfilled every single day.

Finding your life passion often requires the inspiration and guidance of other people in your life. Having mentors during this important work provides many benefits that can open up possibilities where you might not have seen them before.

Mentors may see something in you that you haven't recognized or acknowledged, and shine a light of awareness on it for you.

A mentor has already found the spark of passion within themselves, and they can help you define how your aptitudes and personality might best match your passion pursuit.

Mentors can also inspire you to bring out the best in yourself. They encourage you to believe that what you once thought impossible is actually very achievable.

Whether your mentor is directly supporting you, or you are reading about a mentor whose life you want to emulate, the encouragement from a mentor to find and live your passion creates energy and enthusiasm when hope begins to fade.

Also, a mentor can facilitate your life passion work by offering specific advice and techniques for moving forward. And they can help push you past your perceived limits by setting the bar high and inspiring you to stretch yourself.

Having a mentor, or several mentors, will accelerate your life passion work. When you have someone in your life who is living their own dream, especially if it is the same dream as yours, you will feel empowered and hopeful.

You will be energized to learn what needs to be done and take the actions to make it happen.

Weekly Action

If you don't have a mentor for your life passion, actively seek out someone this week who is living a dream you admire or find inspiring.

Set up a meeting with this person to talk about your life passion work. Ask them questions about how they achieved their dream and overcame obstacles.

Stay in contact with your mentor, remembering to let them know how they inspire you, and how much you appreciate them.

Regularly read blogs, books or articles about people who are living their passions, and make notes about specific actions they did that you can emulate. Refer to these notes often during the remainder of your passion project.

Week 27:
Defining Success

Living a passionate life is often equated with being successful in life.

And being successful is often defined as professional, financial and material success. These things can be the rewards of a successful life, and finding your passion might lead to this kind of success.

But we've been indoctrinated to believe these outer trappings are the only measure of a successful life. Contemporary culture, advertising and peer pressure entice us down a path of pursuing money, prestige and stuff as though these things define happiness for us.

(Refer to the Week 16 lesson for the actual percentage of happiness created by life circumstances and material things.)

Ultimately, we must define happiness (*and success*) for ourselves. If you've lived long enough, you've likely come to the conclusion on your own that money and stuff alone don't bring you happiness.

If professional and financial success has eluded you so far in life, then perhaps these things are extremely appealing. Let's face it—having money isn't all that bad. Maybe your life passion is tied to making a certain amount of money, having a specific toy or reaching a pinnacle in your career.

There's certainly nothing wrong with this kind of success. It affords a high level of freedom, security and self-esteem. But ask anyone who has reached this level of success and they'll tell you—there is a diminishing point of return when in comes to happiness and money.

Pursuing money and prestige for the sole purpose of being rich and powerful will ultimately leave you with an emotional void.

Recent studies[1] on the relationship between salary and happiness reveal that the tipping point is somewhere between $50,000 and $75,000. If you make below $50,000 annually, you might feel stressed about your financial situation and making ends meet. However, if you make over $75,000, the trade-off of working longer hours and having more job-related stress might not be worth the perks. Depending on where you live and the cost of living, there's a sweet spot of happiness potential somewhere in-between that salary range.

---

[1] http://businessjournal.gallup.com/content/150671/happiness-is-love-and-75k.aspx and http://www.forbes.com/sites/learnvest/2012/04/24/the-salary-that-will-make-you-happy-hint-its-less-than-75000/

Another interesting part of this study reveals how social comparison impacts happiness—how our financial situation compares to that of others living around us.

If you make $50,000 annually and live in a wealthy community, you won't be as happy as you would be living near people with a financial situation similar to yours.

Truthfully, the more money you make, the more things you have, the more responsibility you undertake, the more complicated your life, then the less time you have to enjoy the fruits of your labor.

So yes, you might be able to afford fancy vacations, nice dinners out, a second home or whatever you are working hard to attain. But do you have the time and energy to actually enjoy them?

And the bigger question is this: *do they really mean anything to you?*

A more holistic definition of success involves living a life that is happy, fulfilling and meaningful, regardless of financial or professional status.

Frankly, most things in life that afford happiness and fulfillment don't cost much—time with family and friends, meaningful work, new experiences, relaxation time, continued learning and a connection to something greater than ourselves.

Maybe success in life doesn't require as much as we once thought it did. Maybe finding your passion doesn't require a huge leap or a dramatic change, but perhaps just a subtle shift, a refocusing on what's most important to you.

When you define what success really means to you, then you may find your life passion pursuit takes a different turn. You may find you've been chasing the wrong dream. Get clear on what success means to you, and you will clear the path for your life passion.

Weekly Action

Go back and review your life values—what is most important to you in life?

Think about the times and activities that have brought you happiness or given you a sense of meaning and purpose.

Write a definition of what a successful life means to you. Compare that to your life vision.

Make any alterations to your vision based on your personal definition of success.

Week 28:
Emotional Check-In

Just as your car runs more smoothly and
requires less energy to go faster and
farther when the wheels are in perfect
alignment, you perform better when your
thoughts, feelings, emotions, goals, and
values are in balance.

| Brian Tracy

You wake up ready to seize the day, to move forward on your passion
work and the other important plans you have for the day. But then
you notice something.

You aren't feeling quite right.

The sparkle of your mood is dulled or even snuffed out by feelings you can't quite put your finger on. You feel tired or drained of energy.

Perhaps you feel a little blue or lonely—maybe on the verge of tears for reasons you can't explain. There might be a sense of anxiety or even anger hovering around you with no clear explanation.

You want to feel happy and continue on with your passion work. You've spent a lot of time learning about yourself and what you want in life.

You try to focus on the positive, push away the negative feelings, and continue to move forward. But there are times when, in spite of your best plans for happiness, your emotions don't cooperate. You feel like giving up and have little motivation to do anything.

The timing is really irritating—like getting a computer virus or your car not starting on the day you planned your vacation. You've done everything right. There are no obvious reasons for feeling this way, but darned if those feelings aren't sticking to you like a bad rash.

When this happens to me, my first reaction is to fight it like crazy. I start telling myself I have no reason to feel this way. I try to identify the source of my feelings so I can give it the old whacka whacka with my psychological saber. I put on my happy face, say some affirmations, focus on my passionate work, and remind myself of all the reasons I have to be happy and grateful.

Sometimes these things help. But other times a general emotional malaise still hovers around, immune to my most valiant efforts to refresh my happiness settings.

If this happens during your passion work, it feels like a huge setback. It seems as though all of your effort toward finding your passion has been fruitless because you are stuck in these debilitating emotions. All of the enthusiasm and hope you have felt is now painted with a broad brushstroke of despair.

Why do we get these surprise attacks of undesirable feelings? Sometimes the passion work itself can stir up latent emotions. Unexpressed feelings of inadequacy, self-doubt, and fear can manifest in self-sabotaging emotions and behaviors. Even as you eagerly look forward to living your passion, there's a part of you that fears it.

Simply recognizing this scenario as a possible cause of your emotional turmoil can help you turn things around. You can acknowledge how fear has crept back in to throw you off balance.

Exercise, socializing, a change of scenery, eating a healthy meal, meditation, and distraction can help you dissipate these fleeting emotional dust devils. And so can talking through your fears and doubts with a friend or counselor.

If these emotions have been lingering for a while, more than a couple of weeks, you need to pause your passion work and address the emotions. Carrying around anger, depression, or anxiety, will surely undermine your efforts at finding your passion. On-going negative emotions can often be the result of a much deeper, unrelated issue (or sometimes a physical ailment) that is begging for resolution and healing.

Emotional turmoil doesn't need to derail your passion plans. Short term emotional upset happens to everyone -- and it should be expected during this passion project. Long term distress is a call for real action. And real action means seeing a doctor or counselor (*or both*) to help you find the cause, address the issues, and treat the symptoms.

Weekly Action

Take an inventory of your emotions over the last few days and weeks. What is the general state of your emotions? How have you been reacting and interacting with those close to you?

If you've experienced negative emotions, how long have they been with you? Do you see a tie between your emotions and your passion work, or can you identify another cause?

Take proactive measures to change short-term negative emotions through exercise, meditation, socializing, or other uplifting actions. Make an appointment with your doctor or counselor to address lingering negative feelings.

Week 29:
Claiming Balance

Happiness is not a matter of intensity but
of balance and order and rhythm and
harmony.

Thomas Merton

As you work toward your life passion, you become acutely aware of
how complicated, busy, and demanding your life can be. This realization can be extremely deflating.

How can you reorganize all the moving parts of your life to make
room for your life passion? Where will you find the time for this
wonderful new passion once you find it?

There's a fine art to creating your life just as you want it. It requires constant testing, shifting and adjustments to find the perfect balance. That balance involves pulling from the palette of all you *must* do and all that you *want* to do in order to paint a living, evolving picture for your life.

Some days you might need a bit more of the blues and greens, and other days you feel inspired by the browns and yellows. You can mix colors and paint the canvas to suit your circumstances or desires. You can apply broad and effortless brushstrokes or try your hand at deliberate pointillism.

As the creator, you have the ability to plan your painting but also leave room for inspiration and spontaneity. A mix of balance, composition and personal expression make for beautiful art—and a beautiful life.

Of course, it's easy to talk about achieving balance, but in practice it is a fine and delicate process. It's an ongoing creative act that requires daily attention.

Have you ever seen a Bongo Board? You balance on what looks like a skateboard with one single roller underneath. The trick is to shift your balance back and forth so you stay on the board and the roller doesn't pop out from under you. It's hard to stay perfectly centered all the time. You have to continually recalibrate to maintain balance.

I'm sure you see the analogy here. Every day we must recalibrate to maintain balance in our lives. And balance is a necessity when it comes to life passion. Yes, it would be nice to drop everything and focus only on what you love. But that isn't realistic. Bills must be paid, chores done, family tended to. Part of having a balanced life is having a practical and realistic outlook on life and what you can and cannot do at any given time.

Within the context of our existing lives, we must make choices for what is most important and most valuable. If there are several equally important choices, then just pick one and recognize that uncertainty is also part of the adventure of passionate living. Uncertainty shouldn't be a reason for inaction.

Remember, you can do most of what you want in life, but you can't do it all at once. There are about sixteen waking hours in a day, and part of that time is spent with life necessities and work. So we have just a few hours a week of "free" time to create as we wish.

I've found it's far more satisfying to focus on a few things intently rather than cramming in many activities and never feeling deeply satisfied with any of them. If you discover many passions, pick one and focus on it for a while, fully testing and savoring it. You can move on to something else later if you wish. This isn't wasted time, its valuable experience.

When you choose a path or action, take a hard look at your intention behind it. Are you motivated by guilt, obligation, fear or ego? If your intentions are negative, you will likely meet inner resistance.

Sometimes you must proceed because practicality demands it (*i.e. you must do work you hate or fear being fired*). But just having the awareness of your intentions can often take the sting out of your choice. You are making a conscious and creative choice rather than simply reacting to circumstances or demands.

When creating balance and making room for your life passion, a practical first step is to determine the non-negotiable activities of your life. Once you have a handle on who you are and what's important to you, you can begin choosing the on-going activities that are a must for you.

These might include spending time with family and friends, getting a good night's sleep, exercising, working, chores and having down-time to relax. Time for these can be plotted into every day, but the art is in the details and timing.

Once you find your passion, it too will become one of these non-negotiable activities, and you may need to recalibrate the details and timing once again. But that is the beauty of self-creation—you are forever an artist designing your life just as you want it.

Weekly Action

Begin the process of creating a balanced life. Write down all of the non-negotiable activities of your current life and how much time they take.

Then go back and determine your intention behind these activities. Are the intentions positive? Can any of them be altered or removed? Where do you feel you are wasting or giving away time on unnecessary activities?

Week 30:
Coming to a Resolution

Doing this life passion work has the side benefit of developing your emotional intelligence and personal evolution. As you uncover information about yourself, pay close attention to the emotions and fears bubbling to the surface.

Look for the cause and effect between your emotions, your reactions to them and your state of happiness. Complete emotional honesty is essential to self-understanding and discernment about what is most valuable in your life.

The only way to move past the emotions and fear is to experience them fully, uncover the source and address them in a non-judgmental, loving way. Only then do you create the space inside yourself for your life passion to emerge safely, with the added benefit of your full energy and attention.

The source of some of your negative emotions and fears may be unresolved issues in your life. These issues will inevitably hinder you from moving forward on your life passion journey.

You can't be completely free to pursue your passion while carrying around baggage from your past or present.

These issues can include old conflicts left unaddressed or current conflicts that are still heated. They can appear as bitterness, grudges, an inability to forgive or a need to be forgiven.

They might be traumas or hurts from the past you haven't faced, or a reaction to something in the present you are trying to shove down.

They may manifest as an inability to stand your ground, a constant need for approval, or pretense that a situation or relationship is just fine when it really isn't.

Is it impossible to pursue your passion when you have unresolved issues in your life? Not necessarily—a lot depends on the impact the issue has on your psyche.

But anything that stands between you and the ability to have a peaceful state of mind will surely impact your happiness and your confidence that a passionate life is possible. It will be a thorn in your side.

In the short term, it may seem easier to avoid addressing these issues. But in the long run, they will continue to reappear as sadness, guilt, shame, depression or anxiety until you deal with them.

Whatever the issue may be, address it. Clean it up as quickly as possible so it won't infect all of your hard passion work. Living a passionate life requires emotional equanimity and peace of mind.

Weekly Action

Carefully examine your life to see where you might have unresolved issues. Write down the issue(s) and ask yourself what you need to do to resolve it for your own peace of mind. Make note of any answers that come to you.

If resolution requires the involvement of another person, consider how you can communicate with them in a calm and loving way to invite mutual resolution.

Take any actions you can toward resolving the issue, even if you aren't completely sure you are taking the right action. Just addressing an issue once and for all will give you a sense of relief and peace.

Week 31:
Zapping Your Tolerations

I don't have pet peeves, I have whole kennels of irritation.

      ~ Whoopi Goldberg

As you can see, so much of the work of finding your passion involves cleaning up your current life. You have to make space for passion. You have to give it clear and fertile ground to take root. We get impatient for passion to show up at our door, to fall from the sky and into our laps. Sometimes that happens, but it's the exception, not the rule.

Most of the time, finding your passion is a process of peeling back layers, chipping away at the useless, unnecessary, draining parts of your life to clear room for the gems.

You clear room mentally to allow creativity to flow freely. You clear room emotionally to reclaim energy for enthusiasm and action. And you clear room in your lifestyle and priorities to allow time to find and pursue your passion.

Think about it this way: you can't prepare a delicious, beautiful, healthy meal if your kitchen is dirty and cluttered. You'll feel over-whelmed, lose enthusiasm and forget important ingredients. Clear first, then create.

Much of the mental and physical clutter in our lives has been with us so long we don't notice it anymore—like a ticking clock that doesn't register consciously. Even so, it still drains us and steals time. These are things we are tolerating in our daily lives, even though we don't like them, don't want them or don't need them.

Maybe you walk past physical clutter every day, piles of stuff that are distracting and irritating—but you don't take the time to get rid of it. Maybe you're living in a house that doesn't reflect your style or energy, but you put up with it since it's just become the backdrop of your life. Perhaps there are people in your life who don't support you or who treat you poorly, but you're not sure how to let them go.

We tolerate dozens of situations, circumstances and people every day. Most of the time, we are oblivious to these tolerations. We may feel slightly irritated, frustrated or out-of-sorts but not really know why. Or if we are aware of them, we use excuses to avoid dealing with them. It's not that big of a deal. I can live with that. She's not so bad. I don't really have time to handle that right now.

But these tolerations are clogging up your engine. They are slowing you down and getting in your way. When you get rid of tolerations, you begin to streamline your life—empowering yourself to take real action toward what you love, what makes you come alive.

You will always have to deal with some tolerations in life. Some are necessary, and some may be a choice between the lesser of two evils. But awareness and choice puts the power back in your hands. You aren't mindlessly tolerating things that irritate you or sap you of energy. You are making a conscious choice about what you can and can't accept in the new life you are creating.

Weekly Action

Take a few minutes to think about everything in your life that you are tolerating, from large frustrations to minor irritations. Write them down on a "tolerations list," and continue to add to this list as you think of them.

You may notice that some tolerations can be grouped and handled in one or two actions. Others may take more time. Start with the most irritating or debilitating toleration, and write down every possible action needed to get rid of it. Begin taking some of those actions.

Week 32:
Boundaries and Needs

Never be bullied into silence. Never allow
yourself to be made a victim. Accept no
one's definition of your life; define yourself.

⌒ Harvey Fierstein

More than likely, you are getting your basic needs met—food, shelter, clothing, etc. But are you getting your primary emotional and intellectual needs met? Have you identified the personal boundaries for your life where others shouldn't tread?

Everyone has a unique set of personal needs, above and beyond basic survival needs, that are necessary to our ability to thrive as unique individuals. All of our actions and decisions are motivated by our personal needs, whether or not we are consciously aware of them.

Personal needs could include the need to be loved, to be appreciated, to express creativity, to have harmony, to feel recognized or respected.

Your personal boundaries are the limits you create to identify reasonable, safe and permissible ways for those around you to behave, and what your response will be when someone abuses those boundaries.

These can include mental, physical, emotional and psychological boundaries, such as someone invading your personal space, telling you how you should behave, criticizing you or making jokes at your expense.

In relationships, we often unconsciously attempt to get our needs met in both healthy and unhealthy ways. If we need more affection, space or validation, sometimes we seek this without fully communicating our desires. We do this with our spouse, partner and even our friends.

We bumble around feeling needy, smothered or frustrated without awareness of why or how to address or change it. Many people feel uncomfortable asking for what they need and expressing their personal boundaries. They submissively allow others to take advantage of them or treat them poorly because they fear rejection or conflict. Sometimes we hope other people will just sense what we want and provide it unsolicited.

But you already know from experience that this rarely happens. Even our closest loved ones aren't mind readers. It takes regular, on-going communication to honestly share our own needs and boundaries, as well as to understand and honor the needs of others.

Why is it so important to get our personal needs met and our boundaries honored? These desires are what allow us to be our true selves and to feel safe, respected, loved and valued.

Expressing your needs isn't a sign of weakness. It's a demonstration of self-confidence and integrity. You are telling those around you who you are and what is important and valuable to you—in an assertive, but non-aggressive, way.

Setting boundaries with those around you isn't mean or selfish. It is a show of self-respect and dignity, defining exactly where you draw the line within your personal operating system.

When you feel emotionally or intellectually deprived of your needs, you can't live the passionate life you envision. Your needs are integral to your life passion.

When you feel used or manipulated, it drains your sense of dignity and self-respect, undermining the confidence required to pursue your dream.

The first step towards getting your needs met and your boundaries respected are to define what they are in your own life.

Once you identify them, you can take the necessary actions to communicate them to the important people around you. Yes, this can be uncomfortable, especially for those used to accommodating others and who don't like conflict or turmoil.

When you express your needs and boundaries, you may get push-back from those around you. This push-back may be in the form of anger, passive-aggressive behavior or even outright refusal to honor your request. Hopefully, your loved ones support you enough to listen and accept the changes and boundaries you wish to create.

It might take some time to enforce your needs and boundaries, but you can get the message across by responding firmly and consistently when they are ignored.

Some people in your life may refuse altogether to honor your needs or respect your boundaries. If it's your spouse or someone close to you, the intervention of a coach or counselor may be required to help mediate the situation.

In some instances, problems with needs and boundaries may require a total change in the relationship or even the end of a relationship.

As you grow in confidence toward your life passion, you will have less toleration for others who don't support your dreams, or undermine your needs and boundaries. It will become easier to define and express them to your friends and family clearly and confidently.

You don't need to fear requiring this from others around you. Those who love you, and truly want the best for you, will respect you all the more for it.

Weekly Action

Take some time to think about your most important personal needs. Write them down as they occur to you, and then narrow them to the five to seven that are the most critical for you.

Then think about your personal boundaries. To help identify these, think about times when someone crossed your boundaries. Write down your personal boundaries and continue to add to the list as they occur to you..

Think about who in your life might not be respecting your needs and boundaries. How can you kindly but firmly address these with that person? How can you continue to reinforce them over time?

Week 33:
A New Model for Living

Success is not the key to happiness.
Happiness is the key to success. If you love
what you are doing, you will be successful.

ᴗ Herman Cain

Do you ever feel you have to squeeze happiness into your life in-between everything else you're required to do?

Once you finish work, take care of chores, tend to the children, get some rest, then you'll have a bit of time to be happy. And sometimes you're so tired or stressed, happiness still eludes you.

In years past, and still in our current culture, the lifestyle and career model requires that we postpone sustained happiness until retirement.

We put in our forty-plus years of work, get the kids launched, save some money, downsize the house, move to Florida, and only then are we finally able to relax and enjoy life.

But what if we made happiness the centerpiece of our lifestyle and fit the rest of our life around it? Better yet, what if our lives consisted of only happiness-fostering choices and circumstances?

Imagine if happiness were the non-negotiable measuring stick for every decision in your life—happiness infused with some passion and purpose.

Realistically, we know that happiness can't be the only variable for every choice in life. Sometimes we must make less-than-happy choices based on responsibility, integrity, necessity or chance. But perhaps it's the place to start. Rather than relegating happiness to the nooks and crannies of our lives, we begin with happiness as our default position and only step away from it when absolutely necessary.

Yes, it is possible to create your life in such a way that you feel happy and satisfied most of the time. Every moment won't be perfect, but enough of your life will be so satisfying that you feel content and happy in general. And when you uncover your life passion, you can activate it in a large enough component of your life that it spills over into all aspects of your life.

So here's the lifestyle model I'm suggesting:

> ⸙ You address and let go of as many negative, drain-ing parts of your life as possible.
>
> ⸙ You design the major elements of your life in a way that provides more happiness.
>
> ⸙ And you implement your passion in some vital area of your life so it provides a booster shot of joy and fulfillment to every part of your life.

What are these major, vital elements of life? They include work, rela-tionships, money and lifestyle.

Each of these life areas should be operating at a high level on a regular basis in order to experience sustained happiness. If you can achieve contentment and satisfaction in all of these areas (*most of the time*) and live your passion in at least one of them, you have succeeded in reaching a pinnacle of self-creation. Why shouldn't we strive for that?

I'm not suggesting this creative journey will be easy or simple. But nothing worth having ever is. There will be moments of excitement and joyful anticipation, and there will be moments of confusion, fear and doubt. You must make some difficult choices in order to create this life.

You may be required to release certain things you like about your current life in order to pursue something you really love for the future. You may face some unpleasant truths or be forced to stand your ground when it feels deeply uncomfortable. People may question your decisions or attempt to thwart your efforts.

But once you begin this life creation process, grounded by self-knowledge and a sense of purpose, you will wonder what took you so long. As your new life begins to take shape, joy and enthusiasm will generate the momentum to carry you home.

Let's dig deeper into each of these life components and see how you can begin the transformation process toward happiness and life passion. As you examine these areas of your life, you should begin to have a clearer idea of where you might find and pursue your life passion.

Weekly Action

What is your view about the role happiness plays in your life? Does it infuse every aspect of your life, or do you have to find time for it? Do you find that one area of your life drains or disrupts you more than others?

Begin to consider how your life would feel if all areas were satisfying and at least one area was passionate. Write down your thoughts and answers to these questions.

Week 34:
Career Satisfaction

Let's start with the raw facts about your career. On a scale of one to ten, with ten being complete satisfaction and one being totally unhappy, how happy are you with your job? If your answer isn't eight or above, it's time to think about what you want to do with this knowledge.

In a 2010 study conducted by The Conference Board, a business research association, only 45 percent of Americans were satisfied with their work (*just satisfied, not passionate*). This is the lowest level recorded in the twenty-two years of this survey.

In this economy, with the jobless rate hovering near 10 percent, many of us feel lucky just to have a job. Risking a sure thing to do something you love feels indulgent, if not downright dangerous.

Why tempt fate when that paycheck is coming in every month? Doing what you love and "following your bliss" seem like concepts for bumper stickers or refrigerator magnets—not for today's economic reality.

Many people feel stuck in their current situations because they don't see way out. They don't see a way to make passion and purpose pay—or at least pay in the way they've grown accustomed to. It feels way too risky.

There are many other fears and limiting beliefs that lurk around the notion of making a living doing what you love, further separating us from the hope of career happiness.

- What if I'm not as passionate about my passion as I thought I was?

- What if I fail?

- What if people think I'm crazy and reject me?

- What if I make my family unhappy?

- What if I have to give up my current lifestyle?

- What if passion and purpose are just wacky concepts that have no real life application?

- What if I pick the wrong passion?

- What if I have to go back to school or get more training?

But consider this for a moment: you spend eight to ten hours a day at your job. That's more than half of your waking hours in a day. If you don't like your job, you're sacrificing half of your day to a state of unhappiness or at best, toleration. Is that acceptable to you?

To help you answer that question, think about this one—what parts of your current life does passion trump?

Does living a life of purpose and passion trump any of these?

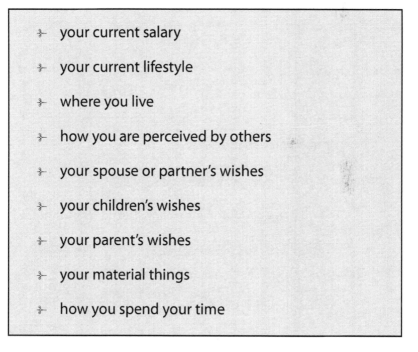

- your current salary
- your current lifestyle
- where you live
- how you are perceived by others
- your spouse or partner's wishes
- your children's wishes
- your parent's wishes
- your material things
- how you spend your time

For me, making a living doing what I love trumps just about all of these things. That doesn't mean there aren't adjustments I can make to accommodate people I love, or that I've had to change everything about my lifestyle. But it means I've chosen to give up some things so I can live differently. And because I live differently, some of those things don't matter as much anymore.

After considering the difficulties and potential repercussions of starting over in a career you love, most people resign themselves to the status quo. There's just too much at stake or too many roadblocks.

But before you give up on finding and living your life passion through work or otherwise, I'd like to present you with an avenue of hope.

First, many of the perceived impediments to starting over or creating a career around your life passion are just that—perceived.

Often we fear things that never come to pass if we begin taking the steps toward what we love.

> ✤ Perhaps you can live with less money.
>
> ✤ Perhaps your spouse will be supportive.
>
> ✤ Perhaps your boss will allow you some flexibility.
>
> ✤ Perhaps you do have the time to take some courses or training.
>
> ✤ Perhaps there is a way to make a living from your passion.
>
> ✤ Perhaps you and your family will thrive rather than struggle through the process.

There are points in our lives where it is impossible or simply not practical to start over, give up your security, and take time off to learn a new skill or even go back to school. Maybe you have commitments you need to honor—to send your kids to college, or take care of an elderly parent, or pay off your mortgage.

Only you can decide when and why to sacrifice passion in your career for the practicalities in life. But (*and here's the good news*), that doesn't mean you have to sacrifice passion altogether.

The restorative and emotionally fulfilling benefits of living your passion in some part of your life will compensate for a less-than-satisfying job. In fact, sometimes it can lead to a career in a way you never expected.

Khaled Hosseini, the author of the bestselling and internationally-acclaimed novels, *The Kite Runner* and *A Thousand Splendid Suns*, began his career practicing internal medicine.

However, his passion was to be a writer and to tell the story of life in Afghanistan prior to the Soviet invasion.

He began writing while he was working diligently at another very demanding profession. But his intense passion for writing resulted in a novel that sold four million copies and generated a feature film.

The success of his first novel has allowed him to write full-time, although that was not his intent when he began writing.

Even if your passion doesn't lead you to a new career, it can lead you to a more fulfilling and interesting life. It can bring a balance and richness to life that transcends your dissatisfaction with your work. And perhaps, like Khaled Hosseini, your passion will open doors for a new kind of work.

Weekly Action

How do you feel about your job? Do you feel fulfilled and engaged in your work?

If you were able to have a career based on something you love, something that makes you come alive, what would that passionate work trump (*reference the list on page 147*)?

What would you be willing to sacrifice in order to do passionate work?

Week 35:
Personal Relationships

Our close relationships are the most important and meaningful facets of our lives. Humans are social beings. We are born needing other people for our very survival. Much of our individual identities come from being connected to others in meaningful ways.

In fact, our romantic partner or spouse, our children, and our extended family and friends are vital to our sense of well-being and satisfaction in life, throughout our lives. No one on their death bed ever remarks that they wish they'd spent *less* quality time with their loved ones.

Research even suggests that relationships are as vital to our health as good nutrition and regular exercise, perhaps even more so.

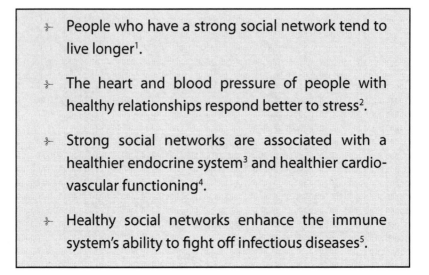

- People who have a strong social network tend to live longer[1].

- The heart and blood pressure of people with healthy relationships respond better to stress[2].

- Strong social networks are associated with a healthier endocrine system[3] and healthier cardiovascular functioning[4].

- Healthy social networks enhance the immune system's ability to fight off infectious diseases[5].

We know intuitively that people in supportive, loving relationships are more likely to feel healthier, happier and more satisfied with their lives, and less likely to have mental or physical health problems or to do things that are bad for their health.

If our relationships are so valuable and beneficial for us, why do we so often take them for granted or just plain abuse them? Why do we save our most hurtful words for those closest to us?

1. Berkman, L.F. "The role of social relations in health promotion." Abstract. Psychosomatic Medicine: Journal of Biobehavioral Medicine (May 1, 1995) 57:245-54.

2. Broadwell, Sherry D., and Light, Kathleen C. "Family support and cardiovascular responses in married couples during conflict and other interactions." Abstract. International Journal of Behavioral Medicine 40-63 (Volume 6, Number 1, 1999). doi: 10.1207/s15327558ijbm0601_4.)

3. Teresa E. Seeman, Peter A. Charpentier, Lisa F. Berkman, Mary E. Tinetti, Jack M. Guralnik, Marilyn Albert, Dan Blazer, and John W. Rowe. "Predicting Changes in Physical Performance in a High-Functioning Elderly Cohort: MacArthur Studies of Successful Aging." Journal of Gerontology M97-M108 (Volume 49, Issue 3, 1994). doi: 10.1093/geronj/49.3.M97.

4. Uchico, B.N., Cacioppo, J.T., Kiecolt-Glaser, J.K. (1996). The relationship between social support and physiological processes: A review with emphasis on underlying mechanism and implications for health. Psychological Bulletin, 119, 448-531.

5. Cohen S, Doyle WJ, Skoner DP, Rabin BS, Gwaltney JM, Jr. Social Ties and Susceptibility to the Common Cold. JAMA. 1997;277(24):1940-1944. doi:10.1001/jama.1997.03540480040036.

Why do we often spend more time on our jobs, tasks, hobbies or just watching television than we do nurturing our valuable relationships? We want a partner, we want children, friends and family. But do we tend to them properly? Do we love them passionately, with our full attention and complete joy?

Perhaps our inattention to our relationships stems from laziness, inertia or boredom. Or maybe it stems from fear—fear of intimacy, fear you aren't deserving of closeness, fear of letting down your guard or feeling uncomfortable.

Sometimes it takes a jolt of awareness to realize how precious these relationships are.

In his book, *Reinventing the Body, Resurrecting the Soul*, Deepak Chopra says the following about marriage (*which applies to all relationships*):

> *What keeps a marriage alive is that you see more to love in your partner; the possibilities grow over time. Intimacy with another person is an incredible discovery, for which there is no substitute. When you find such intimacy, you naturally want more—you want it to grow closer. On the other hand, desire that doesn't go deeper, which circles around repeating the same pattern over and over, has somehow been diverted from its natural course.*

When we put up walls around ourselves or allow distance to develop between us and our beloved, our child or our friend, we deny ourselves the deep fulfillment and meaning that is possible.

Developing intimacy, closeness, trust and passion in your relationships requires your time and attention. You cannot plant the seeds of a relationship and then forget to water it, pull the weeds or spend time in the garden. A passionate relationship (*and not just physical passion*) requires seeing the creative possibilities for growth and discovery, as well as acting on them.

In fact, your life passion can be found in your daily interactions with your loved ones. It can be found as a parent taking care of children. It can be found as a spouse navigating the ups and downs of life with your partner. It can be found as a friend or mentor, loving and supporting others through your presence, words and actions.

Whatever you find your life passion to be, it will certainly involve and impact those around you. Take a look at the relationships you have now, the ones that are most important to you. Don't let them languish. Go tend to them lovingly and passionately today.

Weekly Action

Consider your most important relationships. How would you define the quality of each of these relationships? Are you connecting passionately and creatively?

How would you define a passionate relationship with each of these important people in your life? What actions can you take this week to improve your important relationships?

$\mathcal{W}$eek 36:
Financial Freedom

Our incomes are like our shoes; if too
small, they gall and pinch us; but if too
large, they cause us to stumble and to trip.

~ John Locke

Having enough money is one path to financial freedom. And some
amount of financial freedom is necessary for living a passionate
life. But "enough money" and "financial freedom" are relative terms,
based on one's personal beliefs and life experiences. In general
terms, financial freedom means being free from worry over money.
And that means different things to different people.

When I was first venturing out into the adult working world, having financial freedom meant two things: you made a great income and you had a lot of expensive stuff to show for it. For some, it meant having a modest income but going into debt to get the expensive stuff in order to look and feel wealthy.

During the last half of the 1980s and into the 1990s, the economy had rebounded from the recession of the '70s and was showing an increasingly healthy performance. The United States entered one of the longest periods of sustained economic growth since World War II.

"Yuppies," as we were called in the day (*young upwardly mobile professionals*), were spending their high professional salaries on shiny new BMW's, designer wardrobes and starter mansions. Hair was big. Shoulder pads were big. Homes were big. Cars were big. Salaries were big.

It was all about being seen and showing off. We filled the empty spaces in our lives with more stuff. If we didn't have the money to keep up with the Joneses, we lived with anxiety and the longing to prove our value by working ever harder to make more money. Many of us spent beyond our means and built up debt because we felt entitled to the lifestyle.

In recent years, this wealth attitude has shifted—or has been forced to shift.

I don't know what came first, a mass existential crisis leading to an economic breakdown or an economic breakdown leading to a mass existential crisis. World events—9/11, war, tsunamis, floods, mass murders, global climate change, financial collapse and the constant influx of information we receive through the Internet—have all contributed to a whirlwind of emotional upheaval and confusion.

We've been forced to ask ourselves, *"What is real, what's important, how can I be happy in this scary and uncertain world?"*

As a result, it appears the meaning of wealth and financial freedom has begun to change. But in my opinion it has not just changed, it's evolving to a higher state of consciousness, allowing us more time and emotional energy to pursue authentic passions.

This evolved notion of wealth can be measured in terms of:

- enjoyment of life

- quality time with family and friends

- work/life balance

- travel and experiences

- culture and learning

- personal growth

- contribution

- meaning and fulfillment

- enjoying and appreciating nature

- living a healthy, active lifestyle

It takes some money to accomplish this kind of life, but it does not take ridiculous financial wealth. Nor does it require many material things. In fact, material things often get in the way of the pursuit of life passion.

Seeing the world through new eyes—more appreciative and contented eyes—allows us to take full pleasure in all that we have available to us *right now*. Or we can spoil that by constantly wishing for more.

At the root of spending problems and money angst is a core belief that there just isn't enough to go around. But deep inside we know this isn't true. There is abundance all around us if we choose to see it.

We can erase much of our pain and fear around money by simply reframing our *desire for having more of what we want* to one of *enjoying more of what we have*. Yes, there are people truly suffering financially in the world, but most of us have everything we need and much of what we want. Yet we continue to struggle with money—either desiring more or never having enough of it.

At the most basic level, what we really want from money is security and freedom. We want the security that our most basic needs will be met. And we want freedom from fear about money in order to pursue what makes us happy and what we value in life.

For years, we've been redefining our values to accommodate unrealistic and burdensome financial goals. But perhaps we should shift our financial goals to support our values.

If your life is out of balance, if you are stressed out and chasing your tail, if you are in debt or never getting ahead, if you can never have enough money and live in fear that it will disappear—examine how your lifestyle choices, your spending habits and your financial decisions reflect your core values. You may find that financial freedom is available to you right now if you choose to claim it.

Weekly Action

Where are you now financially? Are you in debt? Do you spend on impulse or to satisfy an emotional urge? Do you live in fear that you won't have enough money?

Are your financial habits and lifestyle in alignment with your core values? How do you define financial freedom for yourself?

Write down your answers to these questions.

Week 37:
Lifestyle Painting

If your life were a painting, step back from it as an impartial viewer and tell me what you see. Do the colors work together? Is there balance in the composition? What story does the painting tell? How does your current lifestyle look to you?

Your lifestyle is the big picture reflecting who you are. And you should be the painter and the viewer, constantly assessing and refining your work of art.

It includes many various moving parts assembled from the multitude of conscious and unconscious decisions you've made over a lifetime. These moving parts are operating within your career and finances, your close relationships, and how you interact with your family and friends. Your lifestyle is reflected in your home, the city where you live, the things you own and how you spend your free time. Even your spiritual and intellectual pursuits, your attitudes and your daily habits are part of your lifestyle.

Unfortunately, most of us aren't very serious lifestyle artists. Huge chunks of our lifestyle evolve unconsciously or with very little attention and input from us. We land in a certain city because we were born there or our career forced us there. We spend time with a group of people because we are thrown together with them through children or work. We have habits or beliefs adopted from our parents without ever questioning them or testing others.

Yes, we do make some choices consciously or even creatively. But there are dozens of reactive decisions we make and mindless actions we take every day. We are reactive because we are uninspired or directionless. Or we're over-scheduled, overwhelmed and distracted. And sometimes we stay in this reactive mode because we don't believe we have a choice. We don't see the paintbrush is actually in our own hands.

But we do have a choice. We can create and recreate our lives many times over. Simply the awareness that it's possible to be the creator of your life opens up a huge emotional space to discover new ways to shift and change. This awareness forces us look at our lives with a truly discerning eye to see where we need to alter the composition and color of our various lifestyle elements.

Once we recognize what we don't like about the design of our lifestyle—where things are out-of-balance or poorly rendered—the blinders are finally lifted from our eyes. A less-than-beautiful painting is no longer acceptable. We must change so that passion can appear, and we have the room available to pursue it.

We may have just a few lifestyle elements that need fine tuning, or we might need a complete overhaul. We may have areas where we are downright unhappy or woefully uninspired in our lives. And we likely have areas where we simply lack awareness or attention— places we simply haven't tended in a long time, if ever at all.

If your lifestyle is choked with extraneous stuff, or unbalanced with work and commitments, you can't have a clear picture of what makes you come alive. How can you come alive when you can't breathe? How can you see your passion through that mountain of distractions and unnecessary time-sucks?

There may be aspects within your current lifestyle where your passion is simmering beneath the surface, waiting to be examined and explored. But you haven't stepped back far enough to see this for yourself. You've been on auto-pilot. You've been distracted and unfocused.

As you begin to clear the clutter from your life, look carefully at what is left and what's been hiding in the dark corners for so long. Allow yourself to examine and explore these things that have now reclaimed your attention or interest.

Let ideas or dreams that you once shelved roll around in your brain. You may find that hobbies you never fully pursued have resurfaced, generating new enthusiasm. You might discover you really want to live near the ocean and write that book after all. You may find you are ready to take that course, get serious about exercise or redecorate your house.

Now is the time to pick up that paintbrush. Start with a new canvas, and create a more harmonious balance in the composition of your lifestyle. Yes, a new creation does involve letting some things go. It does mean challenging yourself, your choices and your beliefs, while experimenting with new ones.

But once you create balance and refinement in your life, you will also create room for passion to reveal itself. Once that happens, there's no looking back.

Weekly Action

Mentally step back from your lifestyle and look at it from a viewer's perspective. Does the entire picture seem balanced and beautiful?

Take a look at each individual element of your lifestyle (*as listed in this chapter*) and decide where change is in order.

Begin to think about parts of your lifestyle that you need to revisit for further exploration. Think about dreams you once had, pursuits you let go.

Do you feel any whisperings of passion? Write down your thoughts.

Week 38:
Simplifying

As you simplify your life, the laws of the
universe will be simpler; solitude will not be
solitude, poverty will not be poverty, nor
weakness weakness.

～ Henry David Thoreau

Now that you've looked more closely at the four key areas of your life—work, relationships, finances and lifestyle—let's begin the work of simplifying each of them to clear space for your passion.

Everyone can benefit from simplifying their lives. We all give away precious time and energy to neutral, mind-numbing, adrenaline-fueling, inertia-supporting, success-stalling behaviors and thoughts.

In addition to making room for passion, simplifying allows us to reclaim time, energy, money, emotions, beliefs and relationships. It helps us create balance and a harmonious synergy between all of the elements of our lives.

Simplifying your life is not something that happens overnight or even in a week. Some areas of your life might clean up quickly. But others will require careful planning, communication and many action steps.

You begin by deciding what you don't want in your life any longer and prioritizing the things you do want.

Creating a life that is totally streamlined and balanced will be a work in progress. As you proceed through this work—as your life becomes leaner and more focused with vision and purpose—you will begin to uncover your life passion.

During the simplifying process, remember to keep your core values in mind. When possible or appropriate, use your values as a bench-mark for making decisions.

As you remove things from your life, shift priorities or make changes, ask yourself, *"Does this support and align with one or more of my values?"* This will help you have added clarity around your choices.

Begin the simplifying process with the easiest parts first. Simplify where it seems obvious and tangible. Clearing clutter and extraneous stuff from your home is a great place to begin the process. As you create space and order in your home, you will create space and order in your psyche.

By determining the material possessions that are worth keeping, you are redefining what is meaningful to you and physically separating yourself from what is no longer meaningful.

Releasing material things makes you aware of attachments that no longer serve you. Begin to see the correlation between unnecessary material attachments and the attachments you no longer need in other areas of your life—to debt, to unhealthy relationships, to poor lifestyle choices.

The process of releasing can be scary and painful. Even when you know something no longer serves you, it's hard to let go of the safe and familiar. This is especially true when you prioritize the elements of your life that you like or enjoy.

To truly simplify your life, you must focus on a few things with intensity rather than spreading yourself thin and never having time to really savor what you are doing.

The feeling of being rushed, overwhelmed or stressed will sap the joy from any experience. You can enjoy many things over the course of your lifetime, but you can't enjoy them all at once.

Clearing out the unnecessary and prioritizing the rest opens space for digging deeper into each element of your life. You may discover your passion is within the depths of an existing area of interest—one that you haven't had the time to pursue in the past.

Or you may find that simplifying gives you more time and energy to explore and experiment in areas you've never pursued.

If you want to find your passion, first simplify your life so you create the time, space and energy to seek it. Your passion needs plenty of room and attention in order to take root and grow.

Weekly Action

This week focus on simplifying your own life.

Consider beginning by clearing clutter and unnecessary things from your home. Give away items you no longer use.

Then mentally review your work, relationships, finances and areas of your lifestyle. Where is there clutter in these areas that is holding you back or draining your energy?

Are there any actions you can take this week to clear up that clutter or simplify those areas?

Week 39:
Choosing the Status Quo

The process of clearing and simplifying will bring you face to face with some difficult decisions.

You will acknowledge areas that clearly need to be changed or eliminated in your life. Then you'll ponder various ways to make that happen and what the possible results and repercussions will be if you do.

There are times or seasons of life when simplifying one area pulls a thread that has negative consequences in one or more areas of your life.

Sometimes you can live with those negative consequences—the positive outcome is more compelling than the negative fallout.

But other times you can't live with them—the fallout is too intense or the repercussions would be too painful.

Maybe you hate your job, but your financial circumstances are too precarious to leave it or make a change right now. Maybe you know a relationship isn't working, but letting it go now would hurt too many others in a way you can't live with. Maybe you want to move, but the poor housing market will force you to take a big financial hit, one you aren't willing to take.

When the eye doctor checks your eyes, she flashes a series of letters in your vision and asks you to compare one set to the next. *"What looks more clear, this (flash) or this (flash)?"*

Sometimes it's perfectly obvious which set is best. Sometimes the difference is subtle. You have to look carefully to discern which set of letters work best for your vision. And there are times when you can't tell any difference, so you just choose one.

You must make the same kind of choices when you are streamlining your life. You hold two (*or more*) decisions in your mental frame of vision. Which one looks best? Which one can I live with or without? Which one has fewer negative consequences?

If I choose to leave my job, can I live with the uncertainty or the financial hardships? If I choose to go back to school, can I live with the time away from my family? Is living in this relationship better or worse than letting it go?

Some choices are crystal clear. Others are more subtle and confusing. But uncertainty should never be a reason for inaction. If you choose the status quo, it should be a conscious choice rather than a fallback position. If you choose change, embrace it fully in spite of your doubts and fears. Indecision causes paralysis, which is part of what has clogged up your life in the first place.

You are the only person who knows what you can and can't live with at any given point in life. Stretch yourself, push yourself and challenge your beliefs about your fears or the potential consequences.

But if the consequences really are too dear, make the best choice that you can live with for right now. You can always revisit the decision later in life. Once you've made your choice, move on and enthusiastically embrace the changes you are able to make.

Weekly Action

What are the areas of your life you would like to streamline, eliminate or change—but you aren't sure you'll be willing or able to accept the consequences right now? Do you feel certain the negative consequences outweigh the positive impact of making a change?

If so, acknowledge this decision as an active choice. Release yourself from the frustration of indecision or regret. Have faith in your own wisdom and discernment and move on to make the changes you can live with now.

Week 40:
Self-Confidence Check-In

Several years ago when I was searching for my own life passion, I remember a day when the emotional walls came crashing in. I'd been working for months trying to figure out what would spark that flame of my internal passion.

Everything I considered seemed either overwhelming or impossible. But back then I had a very limited vision of my capabilities.

I was overwhelmed by despair, believing I'd never find anything that felt remotely interesting. And if I did find it, I doubted my ability to be successful at it.

I began my passion search shrouded in self-doubt and fear. I wondered if I'd been born with a missing piece—the passion piece. My career in public relations felt stale and uninspiring. My skills in

PR were becoming rusty since I was working just part-time while raising kids. I really thought my only other career options were at the mall or wearing a clown suit at a car dealership.

My lack of self-confidence kept me trapped for a while—spinning around in frustration and limited by false beliefs about my marketable skills, my capacity to learn new skills and my fear of committing to something I might not like.

These feelings kept me bound to inaction. But fortunately, I began to pay attention to a career option that kept appearing in my field of awareness—personal coaching. I didn't know what coaching was when I first read about it, but the more I learned, the more it resonated with me.

This tiny moment of recognition—the feeling that this thing may be what I'm searching for—was enough to push me into action. I signed up for a coach training program and took a leap of faith, even with lingering self-doubt. The rest, as they say, is history. I have found my calling.

The irony of this passion work is the way it initially pummels your self-confidence. You're opening the doors and windows in your internal house, peering inside at what hides in the dark. What you see can be enlightening and exciting.

But it also shines the light of truth on who you are now, who you want to be, and ultimately what it will take to get there. It forces you to face the reality that you are fully responsible for creating your life and making the decisions and choices that go along with that.

Faced with these decisions and choices, we feel like a scared deer in headlights. Can I do this? Am I capable of change? Am I too old, too set in my ways? If I find my passion, can I follow through and live it?

Feeling this way is normal. It's the storm before the calm. You are on the precipice of a new life, just about to take the plunge. Of course, you will have doubts.

At the beginning of this book, I mentioned that fear will revisit you several times before you find and live your life passion. Fear will attempt to halt all of your hard work.

But you must keep going in spite of fear. Keep doing this work even when your self-confidence is low. Action is a great cure for low self-confidence.

If you have doubts about your own abilities, remember all that you've accomplished in your life from the earliest age.

You have an amazing capacity to learn new things, to think creatively, to stretch yourself beyond what you believe you are capable of.

Self-doubt and fear are truly the only things standing in your way. When you feel them, remember to push past them and keep your feet moving through action.

Weekly Action

At this point in your life passion project, what is your level of self-confidence?

Are you feeling fear or self-doubt? What are your fears and doubts about?

Write them down, and then next to each one, write down any specific actions you can take this week to help alleviate your feelings.

Then take the actions.

If you can't think of any actions now, fold up the paper with your doubts and fears, and put it in a sealed envelope.

Give yourself permission to keep the fears sealed up until you finish your passion project.

Week 41:
Low-Hanging Passion Fruit

Now it's time for some solid action on your passion project. Over the last few months, you've gotten to know yourself better. You've learned more about your natural intelligence and creativity. You've pinpointed what brings you joy in life and defined those skills that you enjoy the most. You've determined your core values, sketched out a life vision, and outlined a purpose for yourself.

Hopefully, you've begun the process of simplifying your life and prioritizing what is most important to you while maintaining balance in all areas of your life. You've made the decisions about areas of your life you can't change for the time being and accepted them as active choices for where you are now. You have also worked on the fears, limiting beliefs, tolerations and unresolved issues that might be preventing you from taking real action towards your life passion.

So now what? What should you do with all of this information?

Perhaps at this stage, you sense an inner nudging from your life passion. By getting clear on what you do and don't want in life, you're beginning to see the passion that has been there all along.

Or maybe you've opened all of this space in your life and still have no idea what your life passion is. That's fine. It's rarely clear at this stage. But you don't want to leave this space empty for long. Nature abhors a vacuum, and you can easily clutter the space up again with non-essentials in your life.

Let's go back to the four life areas we discussed earlier (*work, finances, relationships and lifestyle*) to look for the low hanging fruit that might lead you to your life passion. For the sake of this discussion, we'll group work and finances together.

Somewhere within one of these areas is your life passion. It may be something right in front of your eyes that you've been toying with for a long time, or it may be something you've never considered (*as coaching was for me*). Your passion may interweave through all of these areas and bring them together, or it may be focused specifically within one of them.

Let's look at each area individually to see where you might find your life passion.

Work/Finances

If your passion is here, you find yourself longing for work that fulfills and engages you. You want to do something meaningful, interesting and exciting that also provides you with enough financial freedom to live a balanced life. Perhaps you are also motivated by making a lot of money, but not just for the sake of being wealthy or impressing others. You see money as a vehicle for living the balanced and meaningful lifestyle you've defined for yourself. And maybe you see money as an outward sign of the energy and passion you bring to your work.

Your career is a huge part of your life, and you are determined to do work that makes you come alive with passion and purpose.

Ask yourself these questions to help you gain clarity:

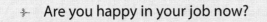

- Are you happy in your job now?

- Does it feel meaningful and engaging to you?

- If you could, would you change jobs today?

- Is there any valid reason why you couldn't change or shift careers if you chose to?

- Are your finances in order with little debt?

- Are you living within your means?

- Can you make the time to do what is necessary to find or build a new career?

- Can you afford to take some time off or a pay cut if necessary?

- Do you think your life passion will be found in your career?

--- **Relationships** ---

If your life passion is within a relationship or many relationships, this means you desire a deep and meaningful connection with one or more people on a regular basis. You draw energy and fulfillment from these relationships.

Your life passion might reveal itself through finding the love of your life, strengthening and energizing your marriage or existing relationship, being a loving and involved parent, engaging in social communities that are interesting or meaningful to you, helping other people, or even loving and caring for animals.

Your life passion through relationships could be part of a career or avocation, or it could simply be how you wish to focus much of your time and energy. Perhaps you will fulfill your life passion by being a mom and homemaker, a stay-at-home dad, a volunteer at an animal rescue shelter, or the person to whom your friends gravitate for a listening ear. Or maybe you've considered being a counselor, coach, teacher or mentor.

Ask yourself these questions:

> ⸙ Do you feel the need for deep and lasting inter-personal connections?
>
> ⸙ Do you enjoy supporting and helping other people?

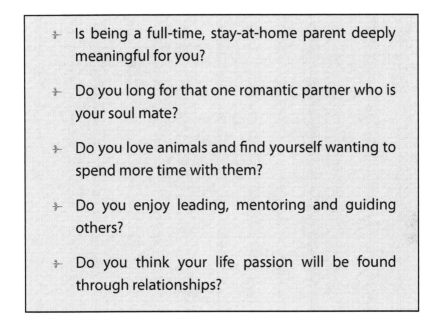

- Is being a full-time, stay-at-home parent deeply meaningful for you?

- Do you long for that one romantic partner who is your soul mate?

- Do you love animals and find yourself wanting to spend more time with them?

- Do you enjoy leading, mentoring and guiding others?

- Do you think your life passion will be found through relationships?

Lifestyle

Your lifestyle covers every other aspect of your life outside of your career, finances and relationships.

This would include your home and the city or town where you live, health and exercise habits, spiritual or religious practices, current (*or hoped for*) hobbies and side interests, fun and relaxation, as well as continued learning or personal growth.

If your passion is somewhere within your lifestyle, you may have a sense that your life outside of work is out-of-balance. Or you may feel the desire for a more interesting, exciting life that taps in to your creativity, intelligence and sense of adventure. A lifestyle passion can evolve into a career, or it can make up for a less-than-passionate career that you aren't able to change now.

Ask yourself these questions:

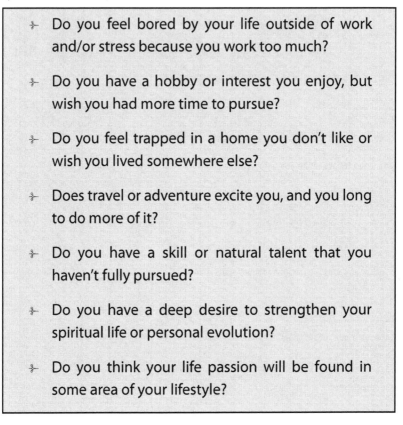

> ♣ Do you feel bored by your life outside of work and/or stress because you work too much?
>
> ♣ Do you have a hobby or interest you enjoy, but wish you had more time to pursue?
>
> ♣ Do you feel trapped in a home you don't like or wish you lived somewhere else?
>
> ♣ Does travel or adventure excite you, and you long to do more of it?
>
> ♣ Do you have a skill or natural talent that you haven't fully pursued?
>
> ♣ Do you have a deep desire to strengthen your spiritual life or personal evolution?
>
> ♣ Do you think your life passion will be found in some area of your lifestyle?

You may find you feel drawn to parts of each of these areas. And ultimately, the effects of life passion will spill over into all areas, even if they don't directly involve all of them.

What you are seeking now is the most obvious and practical place to uncover your passion. This is the time to use your intuition (*which combines all of your life knowledge and experience into an "inner knowing"*). Where do you think you will find your life passion—through your work, your relationships or your lifestyle? Often, the simplest choice is the one you are looking for.

Weekly Action

Review the answers you gave to the questions in each area of your life. Make note of the answers that reveal a strong interest or enthusiasm in each area.

For now, don't worry about the potential limitations or difficulties of pursuing a passion in these areas. Just start developing an awareness of where your strongest interests may be.

If any specific ideas or insights come to mind, write them down.

Week 42:
Finding Your Strong Interests

Life passions begin as seeds of interest. You are exposed to something that resonates with you, and you find yourself drawn toward it. Or maybe you have a natural affinity or grasp for something and over time, realize how strongly inclined you are toward pursuing this ability.

This awareness might have started when you were a child and saw a great singer or athlete and thought, "*I want to do that.*" Or maybe you weren't exposed to a particular interest until you were an adult, but dismissed it because you were too busy or thought it was too late.

We pursue some interests for a short time, but not long enough to allow the seeds to take root. Perhaps we get discouraged or distracted by other life demands, and never allow the interest to fully bloom into a passion. Just because you've tried something before, and didn't or couldn't follow through, doesn't mean that it can never be your passion. It takes both focus and time for most interests to bloom into full-blown passions.

A television commercial during the 2012 London Olympics showed an Olympic swimmer in the ocean with a long distance of water between him and the city of London. The voice-over says something like, *"Olympic swimmers didn't fly to get to the London Olympics. They swam there."* In other words, you don't reach your goals without commitment and lots of practice.

When my oldest daughter was four, I took her to see the ballet *The Nutcracker*. She was mesmerized by the beautiful dancers and sat on the edge of her seat throughout the entire performance. At home, she watched ballerina videos, danced around the house, and we read all of the *Angelina Ballerina* books. I loved dance too, so I enrolled her in ballet classes because she seemed so interested.

When she was younger, ballet was a fun activity. But as her interest and natural ability developed—and as she worked diligently to become proficient—it became her passion. She continued dancing seriously throughout high school and beyond, ultimately pursuing a career as a professional dancer.

You may know many of your strong interests already, but you aren't sure whether or not they have potential to become your life passion. Don't dismiss these interests out-of-hand simply because you are unsure. They could be strong clues to your passion and require your further attention or research.

We have some interests and abilities we take for granted, not recognizing them as anything important or valuable. A natural personality trait or habitual behavior may seem like nothing special to you, but it could be the doorway to something amazing in your life. For example, I've always been a good listener and the friend others came to for support and advice. I felt engaged and purposeful when I was helping people, but I didn't see this as a marketable skill—just something nice that we all do for our friends.

But now I realize these abilities aren't natural for everyone. Active listening and intuitive support are necessary skills for my work as a coach and personal development blogger. These aptitudes appeared in my Myers Briggs personality scores and other skills assessments, ultimately leading me to coaching as a potential career.

Pay close attention to your own personality traits and the day-to-day inclinations and behaviors you might take for granted. Are you a listener? A natural leader? An organizer? The social coordinator? What may seem like nothing to you could be a marketable skill or at least a clue to your life passion.

One way to reveal additional interests you may not be aware of is through an interest inventory assessment, like the Strong Interest Inventory. This assessment has 291 items, each asking you to determine your preference from five possible responses. It measures interests only—not personality or aptitudes—and shows you how your interests compare to people in different career fields with similar interests. (*You can find the test online for a small fee.*) Your Strong Interest Inventory results provide a more thorough insight into your interests and how they might translate in your daily life.

Before you can find passion, you must have inclination and interest. And to know your own interests and inclinations, you need some level of exposure to them, either through testing or real life experience. Getting clear on all of your strong interests provides an extensive menu for identifying what you really want in life, what sparks your imagination and desire, and ultimately what compels you to investigate further.

Weekly Action

This week focus on creating a list of all of your strong interests. Begin by writing down the interests you know off the top of your head.

Then dig deeper to think about your personality traits, how you interact with others, what everyday tasks you find engaging, and how these might have slipped your attention as possible areas of strong interest.

Take the Strong Interest Inventory or find a free interest assessment online to help you find other areas you may not remember or realize.

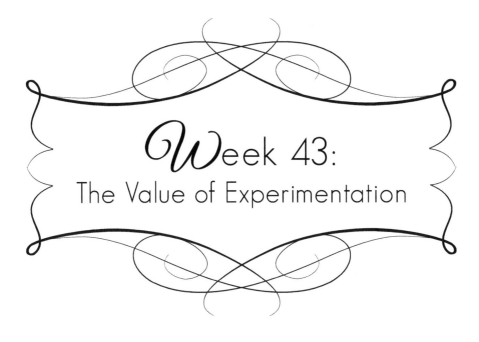

Week 43:
The Value of Experimentation

Negative results are just what I want.
They're just as valuable to me as positive
results. I can never find the thing that does
the job best until I find the ones that don't.

         ℭ Thomas A. Edison

Imagine you are single, and you've just been introduced to an amazing person, a potential romantic partner. The chemistry is definitely there, and the more you learn about this person, the more excited you feel about the possibility that he or she could be *the one*.

So after this initial meeting, what do you do next? The most obvious answer is to go out with them again. You spend time with the person to see if the initial infatuation has more substance, if there is a real attraction between you.

As time goes on, if you keep seeing one another, you may bump into some difficulties. There may be aspects of the relationship that aren't perfect, but you balance those against everything good about the person and the relationship. You decide to make compromises in your life, change some behaviors or adjust your lifestyle in order to have this person in your life.

There are also times when you meet someone new and the chemistry isn't quite as strong. You're interested, but you aren't sure if this is the person you are meant to be with for life. But still, you invest some time in the relationship to find out more. Maybe after a couple of dates, you realize it isn't right for you. Or maybe your learn more about the person, and this intrigues or excites you enough that you continue spending time with them.

In either case, after the first meeting you would never say to yourself, "This person seems really wonderful, and I'm attracted to him or her. But I'm not 100 percent sure this is the love of my life. So I'm not going to go out on a date. I don't want to take that risk."

How would you ever find your true love if you didn't take the risk of spending time with the person who interests you?

Many people give up on life passion before they ever get started. They assume their life passion must present itself at the door with a certified confirmation letter. But that level of certainty doesn't happen. Finding your life passion is like finding the love of your life.

You have to kiss a lot of frogs before you find your handsome prince or beautiful princess. You have to experiment and test.

The experimentation process requires different actions depending on your passion pursuit. But it is a necessary step toward finding your life passion, regardless of the area of your life in which you seek it.

Experimentation can involve research and reading. It involves learning more about your passion from others who are experts in it. It involves understanding the steps involved in mastering or becoming proficient in your passion pursuit. It also might require testing the waters of a particular interest by volunteering, taking an introductory class, being an intern or shadowing someone proficient in the pursuit.

When I was considering a coaching career, I researched and read about the career and training options online. I learned what was involved in training, certification and building a business. I went to a workshop led by a coach to see coaching in action. I signed up for an introductory class before committing to the full curriculum. And I had a coach myself during the process of coach training.

The day I enrolled in the training program, I still didn't know with complete certainty that this was my passion. That certainty came over time. But after all of my research and self-work, it felt like the best option to pursue.

Ultimately, coaching led me to blogging—which required another set of experiments and tests before I committed to it being a part of my life passion mix. Actually, I learned that neither coaching nor blogging are truly my life passion. My passion is helping people create better lives. Coaching and blogging are two great vehicles I use for pursing my passion that involve many of my other strong interests (*writing, design, interacting with people, listening, etc.*).

Prior to making a commitment to coaching and blogging, I experimented with many other strong interests and potential passions. I spent some time (*several months*) pursuing each of these, only to learn for one reason or another they weren't a good fit for me and my life.

You must be willing to put the time into the "dating" phase of finding your life passion before you can make a commitment to *the one*. It's possible your passion may strike you like a thunderbolt, with a strong level of certainty that THIS IS IT. But more than likely, it will happen gradually, as it did for me. Either way, it is prudent to spend time learning as much as possible about your passion.

If you are starting from scratch with a pursuit in which you have little or no expertise, the learning curve will cause some frustration. Your lack of proficiency might deter you during the experimentation phase, but don't let it. Spend time with those who are proficient so you can gauge your excitement and interest, and embrace the process of learning as it helps foster your self-esteem and confidence. Anything worth having involves an investment in time.

Through your testing and experimentation, you will eliminate some possibilities quickly. Others may take more time and research. But don't give up until you are sure the pursuit truly doesn't interest you, or you know without a doubt that it's not a viable pursuit for your life.

Don't give up because of fear, lethargy or uncertainty. You will not be certain about a life passion until you've spent some time with it. And even then, we often have to take a leap of faith to know for sure.

Weekly Action

Begin the experimentation phase of your passion search. Select one or more strong interests and start reading and researching to learn more.

Find someone who is good at this interest and ask them questions.

If your interest is piqued further, commit some time to the pursuit in an informal way (*if possible*) to see how it feels for you.

Week 44:
Finding Your Cluster

There is no such thing as a self-made man.
You will reach your goals only with the
help of others.

⟜ George Shinn

We humans are social creatures. We like being around other people, and we particularly like being around other people who like the same things we like.

Surrounding oneself with like-minded people—people in our "cluster"—makes us feel connected to something larger than ourselves. It validates that who we are and what is meaningful to us actually matters in the larger scheme of things.

What connects people in a cluster or tribe is their common commitment to a calling or interest, and a high level of enthusiasm and curiosity for what they are doing.

Spending time with your cluster helps you determine whether a particular strong interest has potential as your life passion. You are able to watch others involved in this interest, observing how it impacts them and their lives.

You get a feel for how a particular tribe of people with similar passions interact, and how they support and motivate each other.

Having a tribe who shares in your interests and passions can provide a tremendous boost of self-confidence to motivate you during the experimentation phase, and even while taking specific actions toward bringing your passion to life.

This is particularly important if your passion work is solitary—if you are a writer, visual artist or starting a home-based business, for example. You can feel isolated and disconnected, with little to measure your feelings and accomplishments against.

A tribe of like-minded people can provide the social support, feedback and inspiration you need as you work toward your particular goals.

In fact, as computer technology continues to evolve, more and more "real-life" jobs and activities are becoming virtual pursuits. We are spending less time in face-to-face encounters and more time isolated behind a screen.

But humans aren't wired for constant solitary work or play. We need the synergy, emotional connections and sense of validation that comes from personal interactions.

The members of your cluster don't necessarily need to be your best friends. You have your passion in common, and likely some important values, but that doesn't mean you must have everything in common.

What's important here is the affirmation and validation you receive from knowing others share your passion, as well as the practical benefits of being around these people. With them, you can exchange ideas, get feedback, compare methods and celebrate accomplishments. Also the creative energy of your cluster can inspire you to your greatest efforts or achievements.

The dynamic nature of a synergistic group allows the members to focus on each person's strengths and particular talents, fostering the identity of each member to create a more powerful whole. This is quite useful if your passion is team-oriented or requires partnerships and joint ventures.

Finding a particular cluster of people who share your interests and ultimately your life passion is essential to the full development of your passion—and your personal identity.

Of course, your cluster depends on your particular interests, and you must actively seek out a tribe of people who share those interests. You can typically find them in professional associations, clubs or organizations, social meet-ups, religious organizations and online communities.

If you are an introvert or somewhat shy, making intentional connections can be intimidating. This is the time to stretch yourself, to step out of your comfort zone and reach out.

Even if you aren't sure of your life passion, finding a cluster of people who share your interests will help you determine whether or not you want to follow a particular path. Once you find your passion, your cluster will provide the support, camaraderie and motivation to live your passion to its fullest potential.

Weekly Action

Using the strong interest(s) you selected last week, research possible organizations, associations or communities where you might find your cluster of like-minded people.

Make an initial connection with a person or group and share what you are doing or the passion pursuit you are considering.

Ask questions, share information and learn as much as you can find regarding how this group might benefit you during your passion work and beyond.

Week 45:
Intentional Accountability Plan

It is not only what we do, but also what we do not do, for which we are accountable.

ᴗ Moliere

We experience subtle forms of accountability in life all the time. If you're working out at the gym and a beautiful woman walks by, you'll do a few more reps at the bench press. If your boss asks you and a co-worker to write a report, you'll do your best work to ensure the co-worker doesn't outshine you. If you go for a run with your neighbor, you may push yourself a bit harder than you would if you were alone. Accountability can be powered by integrity, fear, pride or shame, but whatever the reason for using it, accountability works.

It provides the element of tension to get the job done—to make something happen that might not have happened without it. By putting yourself out there in front of other people, you are holding yourself accountable to their good opinion of you. You are setting the bar for yourself, and then jumping up to tap it when someone is looking. But what about when someone isn't looking? How do you jump up and hold on to the bar to sustain your passion work?

The most powerful scenario for accountability is the one you intentionally create for yourself. This is the accountability that will support you through your efforts at finding your passion and making it a reality. You must find a way to hold your feet to the fire. When you are trying to make any positive change in your life—to create a habit or reach a goal—accountability can be your best friend. It's a friendship you need to fully embrace if you really want to succeed.

My friend and master coach Steve Chandler tells the story of wanting to lose twenty pounds. He walked into his office one day and told ten people he'd give them each $1000 if he didn't lose those twenty pounds. in five weeks. He put $10,000 on the line. That's serious accountability. That's intentional accountability.

In a program called *The Habit Course*, which I teach with my blogging friends Leo Babauta and Katie Tallo, we emphasize the power of accountability during the early stages of habit creation. Creating a solid accountability plan is a crucial element of the method we share for sustainable habit creation. Without accountability, we almost always fail at sustaining new habits.

It's one thing to tell yourself, "I'm going to write every day." It's another to tell yourself and dozens or hundreds of other people—and then to ask those people to pay attention, to inquire about your progress and to hold your feet to the fire.

As you work toward finding and living your passion, you will have times you want to give up or quit. You will get distracted or busy with other things and forget to follow through. But if you really want to make this profoundly positive change in your life, then arrange your life so it is really hard to give up. Set up an accountability system for yourself.

How do you set up intentional accountability? There is no one right way. In fact, it never hurts to set up more than one system of accountability—like an additional alarm clock to make sure you get up in the morning. For something as big as a career change, writing a book or selling your house and moving (something that has many layers or steps and that might take several months), consider hiring a personal coach. Big change requires more serious accountability, because you are likely to grow tired, discouraged or bored before the process ends. A coach will keep you on track and moving forward faster than you would be able to on your own.

But if you can't afford a coach now or you have smaller goals related to your passion work, there are several other options for creating intentional accountability. Find an online forum, support group or blog where you can report your goals and progress. You can even use social media like Facebook and Twitter for accountability.

If your passion work is something personal, like spending more time with your children, improving your spiritual life or saving money for a course or travel, etc.—ask your spouse, a friend or a close family member to help you stay accountable. Be sure you communicate fully with your spouse to ensure they are supportive of what you are doing. Be sure you tell your accountability partner or group exactly how you want them to hold you accountable. Do you want to be called out if you haven't followed through? Or do you want only positive reinforcement when you get the job done? This is particularly important with spouses and family members, as you don't want accountability to feel like shaming or nagging.

Having a system of accountability is particularly important during the experimentation and final planning phases of your passion project. These are the times when you must get out of your head and really start taking some serious actions to live out your dreams. Even the most self-disciplined people need some form of accountability to keep the momentum going in their life passion work.

Weekly Action

During the experimentation phase of your life passion search, write down all of the action steps required for testing one or more of your strong interests.

Design an accountability system that would work best for you and your particular actions and goals. Implement the accountability system this week by either hiring a coach, setting up accountability online through social media, or by asking a friend or family member to help you. The strength of your accountability system reflects the level of commitment you have to making things happen in your life. Don't skip this important step.

Week 46:
Checking In with Fear

We are coming into the home stretch of the passion project, and you might be feeling seismic shifts in your life. The new knowledge you have about yourself can't be stuffed back inside of you. Whether or not you've found your passion, you are forever changed. You know the person you want to be and the life you want to live.

With that awareness and the knowledge that change is inevitable comes a powerful sense of resistance. Part of you is thrilled and excited about life-altering changes that are coming your way. And another part of you is screaming to stay put, to stay comfortable in the boring—but very safe and predictable—life you've been living.

At some point on this journey, you realize there is no going back. You are like a tight-rope walker inching your way across the Grand

Canyon, and now you're hovering in the middle with no way to go but down or forward.

If you are feeling any self-doubt and fear, then rejoice. This fear is reminding you that you're stretching yourself, challenging yourself to create a better, happier life. The great unknown opens before you, taunting you with any number of frightening and dire scenarios. Almost always, those scenarios are smoke and mirrors, self-designed illusions that have no basis in reality.

However, this is a good time to check in with your fears and doubts and to weigh them against reality. What exactly do you fear?

Is it failure?

If so, have you failed at something big in your life before?
Do you have a track record of past failures?
What did you learn from those failures?
How can this knowledge help you now?
Do you feel you have what it takes to succeed moving forward?
Is your fear of failure legitimate and based on solid evidence? Or is it general and non-specific?

Is it a fear of making a wrong decision or choice?

Have you made poor or misguided decisions in the past?
What have you learned from these situations?
Do you have sound judgment and discernment about what is right for you in general?
Do you trust yourself?
Have you done the research and due diligence to ensure you have as much information as possible?

Is it a fear of disappointing or upsetting others?

Have you made choices in the past based on what others want for you rather than what you want for yourself?

How did that make you feel?

Have you communicated your dreams and passion work fully to those closest to you? Have you solicited their support?

Do you see disappointing or upsetting others as something you must avoid at all costs? Even at the cost of giving up your dream?

What is the worst that could happen if you upset others?

Can you live with that?

Is it a fear of losing money?

Are your finances in good shape now?

Is your debt paid off and are you living within your means?

Do you have an emergency fund and some savings?

Are you conscientious about spending and managing money?

Balancing your fears against reality is like betting the odds. You take into account past actions, patterns and behaviors. You measure what you have learned and how you have changed. You decide what you can and can't live with.

You correct anything that needs correcting or addressing. And then you take action based on all of this knowledge. Do you have a 100 percent guarantee that you are doing the "right" thing? No. You never will. But then again, the wrong thing might lead you to the right thing in the end.

Change causes uncertainty and confusion. And these feelings breed fear and anxiety, mostly over imagined bad outcomes or problems.

Do what you can to address your fears, reduce the potential for problems, and make decisions based on knowledge. Fear may not leave you entirely, but you will have the confidence to proceed in spite of it.

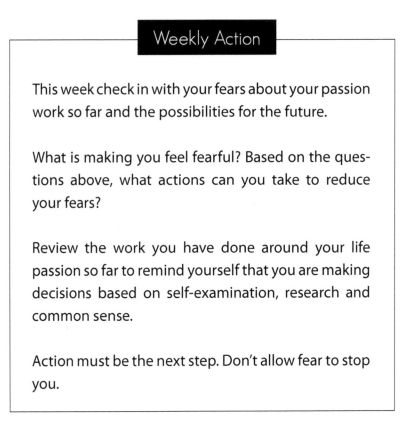

Weekly Action

This week check in with your fears about your passion work so far and the possibilities for the future.

What is making you feel fearful? Based on the questions above, what actions can you take to reduce your fears?

Review the work you have done around your life passion so far to remind yourself that you are making decisions based on self-examination, research and common sense.

Action must be the next step. Don't allow fear to stop you.

Week 47:
Time to Focus

Most people have no idea of the giant capacity we can immediately command when we focus all of our resources on mastering a single area of our lives.

⌒ Tony Robbins

Everyone reading these words is at a different juncture on their passion project journey. Some of you may want to make massive changes in your life to accommodate doing what you love. Some may wish to find more time to pursue a lifestyle change or passionate hobby.

Some passion projects are the equivalent of building a new house. Others are more like redecorating a room. Wherever you are in this project, and whatever your special interest or passion, you must focus on one task at a time to get from where you are now to where you want to be.

If you discovered in earlier chapters that you have beliefs, emotions or tolerations that keep you stuck, then those must be addressed and cleared away before you can move forward toward your passion.

If you discovered that you have skills that need improving or additional training, then your focus must first be on mastering those skills.

If you discovered you don't have the funds right now to pursue what you dream of, then you need to find a way to get the money.

If you discovered you have too much on your plate right now to attend to new changes in your life, then you need to take actions to simplify and streamline your life.

If you've learned that you need to do more research, or experiment with different options before settling on a passion, then you need to take the actions specific to the research or testing.

If you learned that you still need to create a tribe or set up a system of accountability, then that is the work you must do first.

Wherever you are in this process, there is a logical next step. And then a step after that, one after that, and so on. After you have done all of this work to learn more about yourself, your values, skills and dreams, now is the time to get clear on what you need to do next. Every step can be broken down into its simplest form to make it painless and easy to accomplish.

Once you've created these simple steps, the key is to focus intently on each one as though it were the only thing in the world you have to do. Give it your full attention and complete the entire task before moving on to the next one. Focus on each task as though it were a working meditation, allowing you to enjoy the process while working toward the outcome.

You may be very close to accomplishing your life passion, or you may be a year or two away. But remember that each step along the way is a microcosm of your dream. It is a tiny key that opens a multitude of doors leading to your passionate new life. Even if you feel you have a long road ahead of you, it's important to keep moving forward with focused action. Doing nothing and bemoaning the lengthy road will only keep you stuck where you are. Embrace every tiny step while holding on to your vision for a passionate future.

Weekly Action

Where do you need to focus your attention now? Go back through the previous weeks' actions. Are there places you need to refine, tackle further or reconsider? Do you need more experimentation, research or testing? First remove all potential blocks, and then address forward moving actions. Decide what your focus is going to be for this week or the next few weeks.

Week 48:
The Power of Inevitability

That inner voice has both gentleness and clarity. So to get to authenticity, you really keep going down to the bone, to the honesty, and the inevitability of something.

⌣ Meredith Monk

The most difficult part of any action is taking the first step. Beginnings feel overwhelming and intimidating. We try to avoid them and dread the effort and energy we think they will involve. Beginnings require a commitment to the road ahead, whatever that road holds for us.

Our psyches don't like the unknown, so we create an invisible barrier, a closed door that makes it harder to take that first step.

The effort of a beginning constitutes a large percentage of the energy actually expended on the entire action. The stalling, dread, justifying and emotional preparation can drain us before we ever get started. This is particularly true when taking actions to find your passion and bring it to life. There are so many actions and decisions involved, some of which are tedious or unpleasant, that we lose sight of why we've put ourselves in this position in the first place.

But what if every beginning started with an ending? What if the ultimate desired outcome existed before you took the first step toward getting there?

For our purposes here, this would mean you acknowledge the existence of your passionate new life "out there," waiting for you—as a present reality that is simply invisible to you for a time.

If this sounds a bit woo woo, please stick with me for a moment. I'm not suggesting anything magical or supernatural. I'm recommending a change in your approach to taking action toward your passion. Rather than viewing something you want as a goal that must be achieved, view it as an outcome that is inevitable.

This is a subtle shift in thinking. But stop for a moment and feel what it does to your perception of a problem or goal. For example, normally if you had the goal to lose weight, you'd focus on dreading everything you had to do to reach that goal. But if you believe and embrace that a healthy, thinner you already exists, it totally changes the way you think about taking action.

If an outcome is inevitable, then the process is natural. If success is perceived as inevitable—a sure thing for your life—then you will find a way to make it happen. You are "out-picturing" the final result. It already exists. You just have to arrive there. Yes, this does require some amount of faith or positive belief. But this faith actually contributes to success.

In his book, *The Luck Factor*, British psychologist Richard Wiseman points out that one of the reasons some people seem to live lucky and charmed lives is because they expect positive outcomes. They anticipate success, therefore creating a self-fulfilling prophecy.

If you view your life passion as an inevitable positive outcome—it already exists on some level in your imagination. You just have to *set up the conditions* to pull that truth into physical reality. What needs to be done to get you from this reality now to the inevitable reality of your passionate life? Those steps are easy. Use the inevitability factor as a magnet to draw you forward.

Jaime Tardy, who writes the blog *Eventual Millionaire*, proclaims the inevitability of her success in the title of her blog. At the age of twenty-two, Jaime was making six figures. Her millionaire status is just waiting for her arrival.

Atlanta radio personality, Neal Boortz, has a powerful story about the success of the inevitability factor. Before he was a talk show personality, Neal was a practicing attorney. When he was preparing for the Bar Exam, many people—including his own mother—told him not to get his hopes up because most people don't pass the bar exam on their first try. But Neal had an inevitability mentality. While studying for the exam, he shut off all communication with well-meaning family and friends. He knew he was going to be an attorney and pass that exam. On exam day, he wore a business suit to the exam—*as though* he were already a practicing attorney. He passed the first time.

Once you focus your attention on the existence of the outcome, you create the momentum to propel yourself toward that reality. The fist step is creating an inevitability mindset to make your passion real.

Weekly Action

Go back to the vision you created during week 21. Revise and refine it based on all of your learning and experimentation during the last few weeks. If you're clear on your life passion, be sure it's prominently featured in your vision. It's fine if you have more work to get clear on your passion or to clear up some limitations. This work is still integral to making your passion real.

Begin to view your life vision and/or passion as inevitable. Think about it, visualize it, draw it, write about it or make a vision board. Then set up the conditions to make it real by defining small actions to move you forward. Start with the area of focus you defined last week. Write down every possible action and then break those down into even smaller actions. Plot the small actions on a calendar, share them with your accountability group or person, and allow the actions to pull you toward the inevitable outcome. Watch, wait and act expectantly.

Week 49:
Staying Committed to Passion

The most common mistake passion-seekers make is giving up too soon. When it doesn't happen overnight, it's easy to despair that it will never happen. This usually plays out in one of two ways. Either you haven't yet found anything you feel passionate about and therefore believe you have no passion. Or you've found your passion, but believe it's impossible to bring it to life.

When I was going through my passion search, it took two years of active searching and experimenting before I recognized my life passion. I didn't have any direction or guides to help me, so it took me longer than it might have if I'd known then what I know now. Once I embraced that serving others through self-awareness and personal growth was my passion, it took me another year to actualize it in my life with a coaching business and personal development blog.

Even now, my passion is a living, breathing, organic thing that is constantly evolving and leading me on different, interesting paths. Once you land on the familiar turf of your life passion, there are many other adventures that await you if you remain open to all possibilities.

If you find yourself still uncertain about what your passion is, then allow *the process of finding it* to become your temporary passion— in the same way that job-seekers often say looking for a job is their job (*until they find one*).

Be passionate about experimenting and sampling all of the amazing opportunities that life has to offer. Be passionate about learning, researching and observing other passionate people. Be passionate about seeking out the passion that awaits you, even though you can't see it right now.

Think about it this way. You are on a road trip across the country. Along the way, you will stop and visit some small towns, big cities, beautiful scenery and interesting people. At some point along your journey, you'll stop somewhere that feels like home to you. You will recognize it as a place you want to stop and stay. But until you reach that destination, it's totally fine to just enjoy the ride.

If you have found your life passion but feel stuck or unable to bring it to life, I invite you to reexamine all the ways you feel stuck and challenge them. Most of the time, our stuck places are merely the stories we tell ourselves out of fear, projections we place into a scary make-believe future. Once you examine these sticky places, you will see there is very little truth to them.

There also may be legitimate roadblocks, problems that are real and perplexing. But with a positive attitude and some creative thinking, you will find a way through or around them by trying something different, asking for other opinions, or letting go of outdated assumptions. If it is truly impossible to get past these difficulties, then make it your passion to work on addressing them over time. Chip away at them slowly but surely.

If you don't have money for a course you want or a job change, start saving small amounts or take on an extra part-time job for a short time. If you have too many time commitments, begin backing off some of them to gauge the real impact on your life, or ask someone to help you. Very few problems are completely insurmountable if you are motivated to make your life more passionate.

You can also attempt to insert small amounts of your life passion into your daily life, even if you can't make big changes right now. If you want to be a writer then keep a journal, start a blog or write stories for fun. If you want to go back to med school, start educating yourself on the programs and requirements. Take small steps in the direction of your dream, and you may be surprised that unexpected doors open and opportunities become available. At the very least, your days will be more enjoyable and fulfilling as you pursue your passion.

Whatever you do, don't give up—even if you think you'll never find your passion or feel your life is too complicated to make changes. Keep the inevitability of your life passion at the forefront of your mind, and every day take the best, most obvious step toward it.

Weekly Action

Where are you today with your life passion—still seeking it or trying to figure out how to actualize it?

Either way, acknowledge the work and self-reflection you've put in to creating a life of passion. This is one project you should never abandon. The rewards are too powerful and life-altering to dismiss your efforts in order to return to your old life.

You are already changed, whether you realize it now or not. If you are still seeking, go back through your clues—all of the self-work, research and testing you've done so far. Look for something you might have missed or dismissed too quickly. Create action steps for continued research or testing.

If you've found your passion but can't figure out how to make it happen, list five possible actions that can move you forward, even incrementally. Take those actions this week.

Week 50:
Go with the Flow

Life is a series of natural and spontaneous changes. Don't resist them - that only creates sorrow. Let reality be reality. Let things flow naturally forward in whatever way they like.

⌣ Lao Tzu

A very common scenario in personal coaching is one in which the client states an objective or desired goal at the beginning of the coaching relationship, and then by choice or self-discovery ends up in an entirely different place. They may think they are unhappy with their job and want to find a new one, when what they really want is more positive feedback from their boss. They may think they want to organize and manage their full plate of activities, when they really want is to simplify everything.

Opening yourself up to change is like pulling a thread on a woven blanket. You think the thread will pull in a straight and predictable line, but it tends to zig and zag in many different directions.

As you work toward living your life passion, you may find the process is far from linear. But you may still feel compelled to try and follow that linear path, even if a small voice is calling you in a different direction.

Leaving the path you've so carefully planned might mean abandoning your hard-sought passion and negating all of the effort you've put in so far.

But passion isn't always compliant and predictable. If you want to get to the juiciest bits of your passion, then listen to the small voice, and follow it if your heart is pulling you in a different direction from what you expected.

I followed my passion for coaching in a predictable way—by getting certified, starting a coaching business, working with clients and setting up a blog to promote my business. But then I found myself highly attracted to blogging. I couldn't help myself—so I read and researched more about it. I took a blogging course, and ultimately spent as much time blogging as I did coaching.

I could have forced myself to stay on the track I'd originally planned (more training, more workshops, more clients). But I was fascinated with the way I could reach people through writing and connecting on the Internet. It has led me to a very exciting and fulfilling business and lifestyle—one that I wouldn't have if I'd ignored that little voice.

In your life passion process, the goal is to stay focused and actively moving forward, while remaining loose and flexible. Take action but stay attentive to your inklings and interests. Allow your curiosity to take you on a few detours, even if they aren't part of your plan. Some of the most exciting adventures in life are found down the most unexpected pathways.

Our friend Richard Wiseman, author of *The Luck Factor*, suggests that people who appear to be blessed with good fortune share a common ability. They listen to their intuition and pay attention to chance opportunities when they arise. Then they act on them quickly. These successful people are focused intently on their work—but with one eye always scanning for worm holes of possible good fortune.

There is no one right way to go about pursuing your life passion. You might make a B-line directly to it, or you may take the long and winding road. Then one fine morning, you wake up and realize you can't wait to start your day. You feel a level of enthusiasm, anticipation and curiosity you haven't experienced so profoundly in the past. You may find yourself so intrigued by whatever you're up to that you are incessantly drawn toward it.

Life passion often creeps up on you like that. You've been so busy finding it—trying to make it real—that you don't even realize when you are sitting smack in the midst of it. One day you think, "My days are happy and fulfilling. I'm excited about life. This must be what living your passion is all about."

Keep yourself open to all possibilities and inklings, and check in regularly with your feelings about your life.

Weekly Action

As you've worked on your life passion, have you had any urges to take an altered path? Has something piqued your curiosity, but you dismissed it as a distraction?

Take time this week to explore any of these chance opportunities or inner inklings. How do they fit in with your life passion? Do you want to pursue them further?

Week 51:
A Work in Progress

Not too many years prior to this writing, I was primarily a full-time mom and homemaker. I took on a few PR consulting projects, but I had to fit those in-between my daily duties of carpooling, meal preparation and caring for my family. I happily embraced those years of raising young children and being fully available to them. But as they got older and became more independent, I knew something important was missing from my life.

I had always assumed I would gear up my PR business once my children were older. But when the time came, I couldn't do it. I made a few efforts with new clients, but my heart wasn't in it. I suddenly felt like a stranger in a strange land.

What had once been an interesting career now felt like dry toast.

I no longer felt pleasure in promoting other people's goods and services. It had no meaning left for me.

Along with that realization was a huge sense of emptiness and despair. If I didn't have children to raise, if I didn't have a PR career, what did I have? With no idea who I was (*my identity had been my role as a mom and publicist*) or what I was supposed to do with myself, I floundered around for a while with make-work projects and tasks.

But once I set myself in motion with the determination to find my passion, things started to happen.

Over the course of three years, here is what I accomplished:

- Became certified as a personal coach after a year of training with an accredited coaching school.

- Set up a business, developed a coaching practice and began working with clients.

- With almost no computer expertise, taught myself how to set up a basic blog to promote my business.

- Became intrigued with blogging and took a blogging course, learning how to set up and run a blog as a platform for an online business.

- Created a new, more professional personal development blog (Live Bold and Bloom) learning a wide variety of technical skills involved in designing and operating an online presence.

- Wrote hundreds of articles for my blog, guest posts for other blogs, several eBooks and reports.

- Learned how to create videos, podcasts and online webinars to share information.

- Wrote a course on life passion that has sold hundreds of copies, and also created and taught several other successful and profitable courses on self-confidence and habit creation.

- Wrote and published this book.

- Created a variety of successful affiliate partnerships and joint ventures with other online entrepreneurs.

- Served as the editor-in-chief and partner for a popular blog magazine (The Daily Brainstorm) and co-created another blog teaching blog marketing skills (A-List Blog Marketing).

- Launched another expert website (BarrieDavenport.com) helping people find and live their life passions.

- Currently make a great income that allows me freedom and flexibility.

- Provide support, information and inspiration to thousands of people around the world through my online and coaching work.

I'm not sharing all of this to toot my own horn. I'm no more talented or intelligent than the next person. In fact, I began an online business with a frightening lack of computer skills and zero knowledge of how to build my blog business.

But here's the real secret—what I was working on was so much fun, so compelling and exciting, that I was willing to learn and tackle just about anything to be able to continue with my work. Passion is a great motivator for learning things you previously would have never attempted. You'll discover how much you are actually capable of achieving when you are driven by passion.

Finding and living your passion is a work in progress. When you find something you love, something that makes you come alive, you will be carried along effortlessly by your own enthusiasm. You will be highly focused on something that puts you in a meditative flow of action. This is the way it feels when athletes become highly focused, when artists are immersed in their craft—when time and space disappear and you are one with whatever you are doing.

Other opportunities and doors will open for you. Just as my coaching work led me to an online business, your passion can provide you with new and interesting ways of exploring and living it. Your love of sports could lead to a coaching career. Your desire to travel could transform you into a travel writer. Once the floodgate of passion and enthusiasm is opened, you'll be carried away on a tidal wave of creative energy and possibilities.

It is very much like falling in love. All of your cares and worries fade to the background because you are filled with passion. Suddenly, all of the things you struggled with previously—the "what if's" and "I don't know if this can work"—will fall away naturally without much difficulty. That's not to say difficult times and problems won't arise and need to be addressed. Those things will always crop up as they are a natural part of life. But they will no longer dominate and sour your mood.

Occasionally, people find one passion and stick with it for life without deviating from it. But most of the time passion emerges slowly over time, and evolves and shifts as you gain more experience and understanding. Don't be disappointed if passion doesn't hit you over the head. It probably won't. But whether it happens like a thunderbolt or a slow transformation, the result is the same. You will be living a life of passion.

Weekly Action

You have nearly finished your 52-week life passion project. This week, take time to write down everything you've accomplished in the last year, including your life passion work. Look at what you've achieved and reflect on how these achievements have felt as part of a passionate new life.

Have you found your passion or at least something that feels like it might be your passion? Continue taking daily actions to make your passion real, to live it every day if possible. Continue the process of streamlining and simplifying your life to make more room for your passion. Stay aware of your feelings of joy, fulfillment and satisfaction with the work you are doing.

Week 52:
Living with Passion

There was a disturbance in my heart, a voice that spoke there and said, I want, I want, I want! It happened every afternoon, and when I tried to suppress it it got even stronger.

~ Saul Bellow

You know the old saying, "Be careful what you ask for." Having a life passion is like grabbing a comet by the tail. You will be swept up in the power of your passion, sometimes to the exclusion of everything else in your life. When you find something you love, it's hard to stop pursuing it. It's hard to turn your attention to anything else in your life, even other important things.

This is especially true when you first get involved with your new passion. It will be so compelling and interesting that time will disappear. You'll look up and see that hours have passed without even realizing it. When I first began my blogging business, I sat in front of the computer all day (*something I hadn't done previously*) writing and building the business. I'd wake up, grab my coffee and be at my desk at 7:30 in the morning, only getting up when I had to use the bathroom or pick up my daughter from school.

But over time I noticed that I had aches and pains in my back, neck and wrists that I hadn't had before. I was exercising less, my eyes would get tired and sometimes I'd forget to eat. The real eye-opener was when one of my children said to me, "You tell us not to spend so much time on the computer, but you're on it all day. You never have time for me." Ouch. That was a wake-up call. Passion is wonderful, but balance is critical to your overall well-being. You don't want to burn out on your passion or alienate your loved ones in your new found enthusiasm and commitment.

I learned that I needed to stop what I was doing and insert exercise into the middle of my day. I take frequent breaks to stretch and move around, and I force myself to make real life connections with friends during the work day. An online business can be isolating. I also keep regular business hours, stopping at 5:00 or 6:00 so I can focus on my family and personal life.

If you are beginning to make your passion a part of your daily life, you'll experience a bottleneck of critical actions you'll take in the beginning. Your passion may be all-consuming for a few weeks or months. Be sure you communicate with your family. Let them know you'll be especially busy for a period of time, but that after a few weeks, you will have more balance in your life. Then actually follow through with creating that balance.

No matter how much you love what you are doing, we all need time for rest, play, relationships, work and daily tasks. Your passion will lose its luster if it overtakes your life. The ultimate goal is to have a life that works in beautiful harmony, with all components touched by the magic of your passion. If you are doing what you love in one area, you will be happier and more fulfilled in general. This allows you to fully savor everything about your life, even during times when you aren't focused on your passion.

Once you find and live your passion, will life be perfect? Of course you know the answer to that. Life will continue to hand out disruptions and difficulties. But now you have the inner resources to keep them in perspective—without feeling like one more bad thing is being piled on top of an already boring and frustrating life. When you have passion in your life, you are able to view the world from a position of confidence and positivity.

Life passion can begin like a torrid love affair that is all-consuming and intense. Or it can develop like a deep friendship that evolves into true love. As with any important relationship, life passion requires nurturing and attention, especially after the initial intensity begins to fade. You will need to keep the passion in your life passion by continuing to experiment and stretch yourself. Stay open to possibilities and opportunities and follow unknown paths where your passion might lead you.

Life passion is not simply a destination. It is a life-long journey. Once you are on the passion path, you will never be satisfied with anything less.

Weekly Action

Has your life passion or the pursuit of it created an imbalance in your life? Are you properly tending to other important aspects of your life—your relationships, health and rest?

Reflect on how much time you really want to give to your passion, even if you find yourself drawn to it every moment of the day. What actions can you take to restore balance in your life?

$\mathscr{I}$n Closing . . .

Your time is limited, so don't waste it living someone else's life. Don't be trapped by dogma—which is living with the results of other people's thinking. Don't let the noise of others' opinions drown out your own inner voice. And most important, have the courage to follow your heart and intuition. They somehow already know what you truly want to become. Everything else is secondary.

~ Steve Jobs,
Stanford Commencement Address, 2005

Over the past fifty-two weeks, you have learned a great deal about yourself. Whether or not you are living your life passion now, you have done the necessary work to prepare for it. You have laid the foundation to be the creator of your life rather than a reactor to events, the people around you, and your own limiting beliefs.

If you find yourself still uncertain or confused, be patient and listen to your heart and intuition as Steve Jobs recommends. Every day, step away from your busy life, go to a quiet place, and ask yourself, *"What will make me come alive today?"* Have the courage to follow where your heart leads you.

Life passion is not a final destination. It is a daily practice, one that evolves and deepens over time—like a fine wine or a solid marriage. Rather than worrying whether or not you've found your life passion, every day bring passion to what you are doing. Focus intently on the task at hand, the present moment. Practice your passion (*or what you think is your passion*) with intensity and pay attention to your feelings. Ultimately, your heart will guide you elsewhere if you are in the wrong place.

I recently asked my sister, Jesse, to write about her life passions (*she is a therapist, an accomplished martial artist, a runner, and now a cellist*) for an article on my website. Here is what she wrote:

> I've come to understand that my real passion is practice and the experience of flow that comes as its result. By practice, I mean any discipline which allows a person to cultivate themselves over a long period of time.
>
> I don't think school as I experienced it taught me how

to learn. I don't remember having teachers whom I truly respected or ever feeling that I had waded into endless depths with immense joy.

In my twenties, I discovered the Japanese martial art of Aikido. I put in over twenty years of practice, as much as five times a week in some years. I believe I have bowed to a partner or a teacher almost 100,000 times. These are full bows, all the way to the floor simply to begin practice or to thank another for trusting their body to me. I love the unstinting generosity of spirit that practice demands. I love the repetition accompanied by the demand that one deepen, deepen, deepen.

There is a story about a man who approached a renowned martial arts teacher asking to study with him. The teacher asked him why he wanted to learn martial arts.

"To defend myself," he replied.

"Ah," the teacher said, "and which self do you want to defend?"

I have loved coming to know the different selves which have evolved over the years of my training.

Some years ago, I found that the injuries I had accumulated over time prevented me from training any longer. It would be difficult to describe the grief I felt. After a period of what felt like aimlessness, I begin endurance *running. During that same time, I had adopted a child. I came to see that the practice of Aikido, with its fixed schedule, would have been almost impossible given the real-time demands of parenting.*

I was grateful for the solitude of running (and for the fact that I could run at 4:00 a.m. and be home before my son woke up). Again, after some years injuries ended my practice.

Five years ago I began the practice of the cello. The rituals of tuning, rosining my bow, and wiping the dust off my cello have replaced the training uniform, the bows to a partner, and the repeated falls. My teacher reminds me—as my Aikido sensei and my running mentors both did—to relax my shoulder, to open my face, to practice in the spirit of joy.

When you practice in the spirit of joy, you are living your passion. If you want to write, you practice writing. If you want to be an artist, you practice your art. If you want to be a lawyer, you practice law. If you want to serve, you practice serving.

It is the practice of your passion that provides the most joy—beyond success, power, or financial reward.

So what comes next for you in your personal life passion search? It may be clearing up some emotional roadblocks or simplifying your lifestyle. Perhaps you need to save some money, plan for additional education, or do more research and experimentation.

❧ In Closing ❧

Or maybe you have found exactly what you've been searching for.

Wherever you are today, at the end of this 52-week project, you are where you are supposed to be on your personal passion journey.

If you are still searching, your passion is the search. Keep moving forward in the spirit of joy, taking daily actions in the direction of your dream. If you have found your passion, keep moving forward, taking daily actions to live your dream. Your passion will evolve over time, providing endless opportunities for intense joy and deep fulfillment.

If you ever forget why you are on this path to passion, let me remind you . . .

> - Even small changes in the direction of your passion can make a huge difference. You can create enough of what you want for your life to substantially improve your level of happiness and life satisfaction.
>
> - As you work toward your passion, you will get very, very clear on your priorities and how to structure your life around them.
>
> - Your relationships will be better because you are happier and clear about your life. You will be more attractive and interesting to others.
>
> - You will see possibilities and opportunities where you didn't know they existed before and have the willingness to pursue them.

- Your life will be much easier as you are in the flow of what you love. In fact, you will no longer sweat the small stuff, because you are so engaged in what you have going on in life.

- As you begin to live your passion, you will have increased energy and find that time just flies because you love what you do.

- Your self-confidence and self-esteem will improve dramatically because you are taking control of your own life, creating it on your own terms, and living it with a sense of purpose.

- You will come alive again.

The world needs more people who come alive. The world needs people who are excited, engaged, joyful, and living with passion and purpose. We are waiting for you.

You, dear reader, have something amazing to offer the world. Go find it and live it!

With Gratitude

Any passion success story doesn't happen without the guidance, wisdom, and support of others. Mine is no exception.

I offer my sincere and humble thanks to . . .

Stephanie Wetzel, who has taught me that there is no obstacle too great when seeking out your life passion. Her courage, determination, and loving spirit inspire me and many others. She is also the creative genius behind my site design and the design of this book. I couldn't have done it without her.

Steve Chandler, the amazing coach and author who challenged me to write a book. He doesn't know the power his encouraging words had on me, but I am so grateful for his support and mentorship.

Jason Gracia and Corbett Barr, who showed me how to turn my passion into a business, inspiring me with their integrity and challenging me to focus on what is most important for success.

My readers at BarrieDavenport.com and LiveBoldandBloom.com who awe me with their courage and desire to live passionately and to stretch themselves beyond perceived limits. You are the reason I wake up with enthusiasm and purpose every day.

My children, Allyn, John and Diana—just because I love you. Being your mom will always be my first passion.

About the Author

Barrie Davenport is a certified life passion coach who is passionate about helping others find what makes them come alive. She is the founder of BarrieDavenport.com, a site devoted to helping people uncover and live their passions, as well as Live Bold and Bloom, one of the leading personal development blogs on the Internet, focused on personal growth for bold, passionate and adventurous living.

She is co-creator of The Habit Course, a self-study program helping people create and sustain new habits for life; and Simple Self-Confidence, an interactive course for personal empowerment.

She has been featured on various blogs including Zen Habits, Tiny Buddha, Think Traffic, Pick the Brain, and many others. Barrie had a successful 25-year career as a public relations executive and consultant, working with celebrities, writers, artists, and other professionals—but she left this career to seek her true calling as a coach, author and blogger.

Barrie lives in Roswell, Georgia and has three children.

If you are interested in learning more information
on life passion, you can read Barrie's weekly articles
on the topic through her website at

http://www.barriedavenport.com

You can also download her free guide,
*The Passion Myths: 6 Lies Keeping You from
Uncovering Your Life Passion* at

http://www.barriedavenport.com/freeguide/

Connect with Barrie on Facebook at
http://www.facebook.com/CoachBarrie

and on Twitter at
http://twitter.com/CoachBarrie

or via email at
mybloomlife@gmail.com

Made in the USA
Middletown, DE
11 October 2017